Baltimore Orioles 2019

A Baseball Companion

Edited by Patrick Dubuque, Aaron Gleeman and Bret Sayre

Baseball Prospectus

Craig Brown and Dave Pease, Consultant Editors
Rob McQuown and Harry Pavlidis, Statistics Editors

Copyright © 2019 by DIY Baseball, LLC.
All rights reserved

This book or any part thereof may not be reproduced or transmitted in any form or by any means, electronic or mechanical, including photocopying, recording, or by any information storage and retrieval system, without permission in writing from the publisher.

Limit of Liability/Disclaimer of Warranty: While the publisher and the author have used their best efforts in preparing this book, they make no representations or warranties with respect to the accuracy or completeness of the contents of this book and specifically disclaim any implied warranties of merchantability or fitness for a particular purpose. No warranty may be created or extended by sales representatives or written sales materials. The advice and strategies contained herein may not be suitable for your situation. You should consult with a professional where appropriate. Neither the publisher nor the author shall be liable for any loss of profit or any other commercial damages, including but not limited to special, incidental, consequential, or other damages.

Library of Congress Cataloging-in-Publication Data:
paperback
ISBN-13: 978-1-949332-00-1

Project Credits
Cover Design: Kathleen Dyson
Interior Design and Production: Jeff Pease, Dave Pease
Layout: Jeff Pease, Dave Pease

Baseball icon courtesy of Uberux, from https://www.shareicon.net/author/uberux

Ballpark diagram courtesy of Lou Spirito/THIRTY81 Project, https://thirty81project.com/

Manufactured in the United States of America
10 9 8 7 6 5 4 3 2 1

Table of Contents

Foreword v
    Rob Mains

Statistical Introduction vii

Part 1: Team Analysis

Table for Two: Previewing the 2019 Baltimore Orioles 3
    Darius Austin and Kate Preusser

Performance Graphs 11

2018 Team Performance 12

2019 Team Projections 13

Team Personnel 14

Oriole Park at Camden Yards Stats 15

Orioles Team Analysis 17

Part 2: Player Analysis

Orioles Player Analysis 22

Orioles Prospects 95

Part 3: Featured Articles

The Hole in The Shift is Fixing Itself 109
    Russell Carleton

The State of the Quality Start 113
    Rob Mains

Heads-Up Hacking—The First Pitch 119
    Matthew Trueblood

A Hymn for the Index Stat 125
    Patrick Dubuque

Index of Names 129

Foreword

Rob Mains

Welcome to this companion of the 2019 Baltimore Orioles. We at Baseball Prospectus are excited to provide this analysis of the Orioles.

Our website, Baseball Prospectus, is a leader in delivering high-quality commentary and data to baseball fans everywhere. To some, those words—commentary and data—appear mutually exclusive. There are people out there who believe that traditional analysis and advanced analytics must run on different paths. But the simplistic narrative of stats vs. traditionalists just isn't true. Every team's analytics department interacts with scouting, development, and major league operations with a common goal: Delivering a championship. New technologies, like radar tracking of pitch speeds and movement, enable talent evaluators to focus on qualitative aspects of pitching like mechanics and pitch sequencing. In-game strategies like infield shifts, based on batters' hit tendencies, help turn balls in play into outs. Hitters use information to adjust their swings to maximize run production.

All these numbers can seem, at best, intimidating, and at worst, counterproductive to the casual fan. Even as technology and analysis have embedded themselves deeply into the way teams run, it can often feel like statistics create a displacement between the viewer and the sport, breaking them out of the action. And yet every fan incorporates the numbers to some degree; stats like batting average and earned run average, so fundamental to how we talk about performance, are actually complicated formulas. They don't bother people because those formulas have become second nature, as easy to translate as the action on the field.

Along the way, new statistics have entered baseball's lexicon. You'll see some of them, like on-base percentage (which measures a batter's ability to get on base via walk, hit batter, or hit), OPS (on-base plus slugging), and average exit velocity (the speed of balls off a hitter's bat) on broadcasts. Others, like DRC+, might well be new to you. Some of them have been well-defined to the public, others haven't. That lack of context has created ambiguity. Fans know that a ball hit 100 mph is scorched, but does that mean extra bases? (Not if it's hit on the ground or high in the air it doesn't.)

Baltimore Orioles 2019

For those who are amenable to them, the new statistics can increase the enjoyment and understanding of the game. They can help fans identify when a pitcher is tiring, when a stolen base or a bunt attempt makes sense (and, more often, when it doesn't), or how a team's lineup might be constructed. Websites like Baseball Prospectus add to that understanding by weaving metrics into the narrative of the game. That's the goal of this publication: to take some of the newer, more complicated statistics and make them as intuitive as the ones on the back of old baseball cards.

But you don't need to love analytics to love baseball. The fans at BP who worked together to write this guide are captivated first and foremost by the game itself. We're drawn to Aaron Judge's power, Francisco Lindor's glove, Billy Hamilton's speed and Patrick Corbin's slider and don't need numbers to tell us why they're so mesmerizing. The underlying statistics provide depth to the game that we all love.

We hope you'll find that this guide helps you better understand the Orioles. Our analysts have studied the team's major league personnel and its minor league affiliates to identify their strengths and weaknesses, both the obvious ones and those that only a careful dissection of players' performances—yes, including the data—can reveal. You don't need us to tell you who was good and who wasn't in 2018, but our models and writers can help you project how each player is going to perform this year and beyond, and appreciate the greatness of each new game as it unfolds. As in the sport itself, the human and analytic components combine to generate a deeper overall understanding.

Think back to the first time you saw a baseball game on a high-definition TV. You'd grown familiar with how the game looked and felt on a picture tube. But new TV allowed you to see details that you'd never seen before. That's how advanced statistics work. The game itself is why you're here and why you're buying this. (And, for that matter, why we wrote it.) The statistical measures provide the sharper focus, the detail, the depth of knowledge that you didn't have before, generating an overall superior picture. Enjoy the view.

—Rob Mains is an author of Baseball Prospectus.

Statistical Introduction

Sports are, fundamentally, a blend of athletic endeavor and storytelling. Baseball, like any other sport, tells its stories in so many ways: in the arc of a game from the stands or a season from the box scores, in photos, or even in numbers. At Baseball Prospectus, we understand that statistics don't replace observation or any of baseball's stories, but complement everything else that makes the game so much fun.

What stats help us with is with patterns and precision, variance and value. This book can help you learn things you may not see from watching a game or hundred, whether it's the path of a career over time or the breadth of the entire MLB. We'd also never ask you to choose between our numbers and the experience of viewing a game from the cheap seats or the comfort of your home; our publication combines running the numbers with observations and wisdom from some of the brightest minds we can find. But if you *do* want to learn more about the numbers beyond what's on the backs of player jerseys, let us help explain.

Offense

At the end of this past year, we've revised our methodology for determining batting value. Long-time readers of Baseball Prospectus will notice that we've retired True Average in favor of a new metric: Deserved Runs Created Plus (DRC+). Developed by Jonathan Judge and our stats team, this statistic measures everything a player does at the plate–reaching base, hitting for power, making outs, and moving runners over–and puts it on a scale where 100 equals league-average performance. A DRC+ of 150 is terrific, a DRC+ of 100 is average, and a DRC+ of 75 means you better be an excellent defender.

DRC+ also does a better job than any of our previous metrics in taking contextual factors into account. The model adjusts for how the park affects performance, but also for things like the talent of the opposing pitcher, value of different types of batted-ball events, league, temperature, and other factors. It's able to describe a player's expected offensive contribution than any other statistic we've found over the years, and also does a better job of predicting future performance as well.

Baltimore Orioles 2019

The other aspect of run-scoring is baserunning, which we quantify using Baserunning Runs. BRR not only records the value of stolen bases (or getting caught in the act), but also accounts for a runner's ability to go first to third on a single or advance on a fly ball.

Defense

Where offensive value is *relatively* easy to identify and understand, defensive value is ... not. Over the past dozen years, the sabermetric community has focused mostly on stats based on zone data: a real-live human person records the type of batted ball and estimated landing location, and models are created that give expected outs. From there, you can compare fielders' actual outs to those expected ones. Simple, right?

Unfortunately, zone data has two major issues. First, zone data is recorded by commercial data providers who keep the raw data private unless you pay for it. (All the statistics we build in this book and on our website use public data as inputs.) That hurts our ability to test assumptions or duplicate results. Second, over the years it has become apparent that there's quite a bit of "noise" in zone-based fielding analysis. Sometimes the conclusions drawn from zone data don't hold up to scrutiny, and sometimes the different data provided by different providers don't look anything alike, giving wildly different results. Sometimes the hard-working professional stringers or scorers might unknowingly inflict unconscious bias into the mix: for example good fielders will often be credited with more expected outs despite the data, and ballparks with high press boxes tend to score more line drives than ones with a lower press box.

Enter our Fielding Runs Above Average (FRAA). For most positions, FRAA is built from play-by-play data, which allows us to avoid the subjectivity found in many other fielding metrics. The idea is this: count how many fielding plays are made by a given player and compare that to expected plays for an average fielder at their position (based on pitcher ground-ball tendencies and batter handedness). Then we adjust for park and base-out situations.

When it comes to catchers, our methodology is a little different thanks to the laundry list of responsibilities they're tasked with beyond just, well, catching and throwing the ball. By now you've probably heard about "framing" or the art of making umpires more likely to call balls outside the strike zone for strikes. To put this into one tidy number, we incorporate pitch tracking data (for the years it exists) and adjust for important factors like pitcher, umpire, batter, and home-field advantage using a mixed-model approach. This grants us a number for how many strikes the catcher is personally adding to (or subtracting from) his pitchers' performance ... which we then convert to runs added or lost using linear weights.

Framing is one of the biggest parts of determining catcher value, but we also take into account blocking balls from going past, whether a scorer deems it a passed ball or a wild pitch. We use a similar approach–one that really benefits from the pitch tracking data that tells us what ends up in the dirt and what doesn't. We also include a catcher's ability to prevent stolen bases and how well they field balls in play, and *finally* we come up with our FRAA for catchers.

Pitching

Both pitching and fielding make up the half of baseball that isn't run scoring: run prevention. Separating pitching from fielding is a tough task, and most recent pitching analysis has branched off from Voros McCracken's famous (and controversial) statement, "There is little if any difference among major-league pitchers in their ability to prevent hits on balls hit in the field of play." The research of the analytic community has validated this to some extent, and there are a host of "defense-independent" pitching measures that have been developed to try and extricate the effect of the defense behind a hurler from the pitcher's work.

Our solution to this quandry is Deserved Run Average (DRA), our core pitching metric. DRA looks like earned run average (ERA), the tried-and-true pitching stat you've seen on every baseball broadcast or box score from the past century, but it's very different. To start, DRA takes an event-by-event look at what the pitchers does, and adjusts the value of that event based on different environmental factors like park, batter, catcher, umpire, base-out situation, run differential, inning, defense, home field advantage, pitcher role, and temperature. That mixed model gives us a pitcher's expected contribution, similar to what we do for our DRC+ model for hitters and FRAA model for catchers. (Oh, and we also consider the pitcher's effect on basestealing and on balls getting past the catcher.)

It's important to note that DRA is set to the scale of runs allowed per nine innings (RA9) instead of ERA, which makes DRA's scale slightly higher than ERA's. The reason for this is because ERA tends to overrate three types of pitchers:

1. Pitchers who play in parks where scorers hand out more errors. Official scorers differ significantly in the frequency at which they assign errors to fielders.
2. Ground-ball pitchers, because a substantial proportion of errors occur on grounders.
3. Pitchers who aren't very good. Better pitchers often allow fewer unearned runs than bad pitchers, because good pitchers tend to find ways to get out of jams.

Since the last time you picked up an edition of this book, we've also made a few minor changes to DRA to make it better. Recent research into "tunneling"–the act of throwing consecutive pitches that appear similar from a batter's point of view until after the swing decision point–data has given us a new contextual factor to account for in DRA: plate distance. This refers to the distance between successive pitches as they approach the plate, and while it has a smaller effect than factors like velocity or whiff rate, it still can help explain pitcher strikeout rate in our model.

New Pitching Metrics for 2019

We're including a few "new" pitching metrics for 2019's suite of Baseball Prospectus publications, but you may be familiar with them if you've spent time scouring the internet for stats.

Fastball Percentage

Our fastball percentage (FB%) statistic measures how frequently a pitcher throws a pitch classified as a "fastball," measured as a percentage of overall pitches thrown. We qualify three types of fastballs:

1. The traditional four-seam fastball;
2. The two-seam fastball or sinker;
3. "Hard cutters," which are pitches that have the movement profile of a cut fastball and are used as the pitcher's primary offering or in place of a more traditional fastball.

For example, a pitcher with a FB% of 67 throws any combination of these three pitches about two-thirds of the time.

Whiff Rate

Everybody loves a swing and a miss, and whiff rate (WHF) measures how frequently pitchers induce a swinging strike. To calculate WHF, we add up all the pitches thrown that ended with a swinging strike, then divide that number by a pitcher's total pitches thrown. Most often, high whiff rates correlate with high strikeout rates (and overall effective pitcher performance).

Called Strike Probability

Called Strike Probability (CSP) is a number that represents the likelihood that all of a pitcher's pitches will be called a strike while controlling for location, pitcher and batter handedness, umpire and count. Here's how it works: on each pitch, our model determines how many times (out of 100) that a similar pitch was called for a strike given those factors mentioned above, and when normalized for each batter's strike zone. Then we average the CSP for all pitches thrown by a pitcher in a season, and that gives us the yearly CSP percentage you see in the stats boxes.

As you might imagine, pitchers with a higher CSP are more likely to work in the zone, where pitchers with a lower CSP are likely locating their pitches outside the normal strike zone, for better or for worse.

Projections

Many of you aren't turning to this book just for a look at what a player has done, but for a look at what a player is going to do: the PECOTA projections. PECOTA, initially developed by Nate Silver (who has moved on to greater fame as a political analyst), consists of three parts:

1. Major-league equivalencies, which use minor-league statistics to project how a player will perform in the major leagues;
2. Baseline forecasts, which use weighted averages and regression to the mean to estimate a player's current true talent level; and
3. Aging curves, which uses the career paths of comparable players to estimate how a player's statistics are likely to change over time.

With all those important things covered, let's take a look at what's in the book this year.

Team Prospectus

You bought this book to learn more about your favorite (or maybe least-favorite, who are we to judge?) team, so let's talk about them. After a thoughtful preview of the 2019 season, you'll be presented with our Team Prospectus. This outlines many of the key statistics for each team's 2018 season, as well as a very inviting stadium diagram.

First you'll find the Performance Graphs page. The first is the 2018 Hit List Ranking. This shows our Hit List Rank for the team on each day of the 2018 season and is intended to give you a picture of the ups and downs of the team's season, including their highest and lowest ranks of the year. Hit List Rank measures overall team performance and drives the Hit List Power Rankings at the baseballprospectus.com website.

The second graph is Committed Payroll and helps you see how the team's payroll has compared to the MLB and divisional average payrolls over time. Payroll figures are currents as of January 1, 2019; with so many free agents still unsigned as of this writing, the final 2018 figure will likely be significantly different for many teams. (In the meantime, you can always find the most current data at Baseball Prospectus' Cot's Baseball Contracts page.)

Baltimore Orioles 2019

The third graph is Farm System Ranking and displays how the Baseball Prospectus prospect team has ranked the organization's farm system since 2007. It also indicates the highest and lowest ranks that the farm system achieved over that time.

We start the Team Performance page with the squad's unadjusted and third-order 2018 win-loss records, presented in divisional context. We then list the three highest performing hitters and pitchers by WARP for 2018. Beneath that are a host of other team statistics. **Pythag** presents an adjusted 2018 winning percentage, calculated by taking runs scored per game (**RS/G**) and runs allowed per game (**RA/G**) for the team, and running them through a version of Bill James' Pythagorean formula that was refined and improved by David Smyth and Brandon Heipp. (The formula is called "Pythagenpat," which is equally fun to type and to say.)

Next up is **DRC+**, described earlier, to indicate the overall hitting ability of the team either above or below league-average. Run prevention on the pitching side is covered by **DRA** (also mentioned earlier) and another metric: Fielding Independent Pitching (**FIP**), which calculates another ERA-like statistic based on strikeouts, walks, and home runs recorded. Defensive Efficiency Rating (**DER**) tells us the percentage of balls in play turned into outs for the team, and is a quick fielding shorthand that rounds out run prevention.

After that, we have several measures related to roster composition, as opposed to on-field performance. **B-Age** and **P-Age** tell us the average age of a team's batters and pitchers, respectively. **Salary** is the combined team payroll for all on-field players, and Doug Pappas' Marginal Dollars per Marginal Win (**M$/MW**) tells us how much money a team spent to earn production above replacement level.

Ending this batch of statistics is the number of disabled list days a team had over the season (**DL Days**) and the amount of salary paid to players on the disabled list (**$ on DL**); this final number is expressed as a percentage of total payroll.

Next to each of these stats, we've listed each team's MLB rank in that category from 1st to 30th. In this, 1st always indicates a positive outcome and 30th a negative outcome, except in the case of salary–1st is highest.

The Team Projections page is intended to convey the team's operational capacity entering the 2019 season. We start with the team's PECOTA projected record for 2019, again in divisional context. The **+/-** column indicates how many more or less wins the team is projected to get than they got in 2018. We then list the three highest projected hitters and pitchers by WARP for 2018. A brief farm system summary follows, with the team's top prospect and number of BP Top 101 Prospects. Finally, we list the key new players and departed players, along with their 2019 projected WARP.

Alex Bregman 3B

Born: 03/30/94 Age: 25 Bats: R Throws: R
Height: 6'0" Weight: 180 Origin: Round 1, 2015 Draft (#2 overall)

YEAR	TEAM	LVL	AGE	PA	R	2B	3B	HR	RBI	BB	K	SB	CS	AVG/OBP/SLG
2016	CCH	AA	22	285	54	16	2	14	46	42	26	5	3	.297/.415/.559
2016	FRE	AAA	22	83	17	6	0	6	15	5	12	2	1	.333/.373/.641
2016	HOU	MLB	22	217	31	13	3	8	34	15	52	2	0	.264/.313/.478
2017	HOU	MLB	23	626	88	39	5	19	71	55	97	17	5	.284/.352/.475
2018	HOU	MLB	24	705	105	51	1	31	103	96	85	10	4	.286/.394/.532
2019	HOU	MLB	25	675	96	38	3	23	78	73	107	12	4	.272/.359/.463

Breakout: 6%   Improve: 52%   Collapse: 5%   Attrition: 2%   MLB: 100%
Comparables: Anthony Rendon, David Wright, Pablo Sandoval

YEAR	TEAM	LVL	AGE	PA	DRC+	VORP	BABIP	BRR	FRAA	WARP
2016	CCH	AA	22	285	172	38.9	.286	1.6	SS(51): -3.4, 3B(11): 1.4	2.7
2016	FRE	AAA	22	83	161	10.0	.333	-1.2	SS(14): 2.1, LF(3): -0.1	0.8
2016	HOU	MLB	22	217	107	9.6	.317	0.5	3B(40): 0.9, SS(6): -0.1	1.1
2017	HOU	MLB	23	626	114	34.7	.311	-1.5	3B(132): 8.7, SS(30): -2.9	3.9
2018	HOU	MLB	24	705	150	72.6	.289	-1.6	3B(136): 5.4, SS(28): -0.4	7.4
2019	HOU	MLB	25	675	125	37.3	.295	0.0	3B 7, SS 0	4.6

After the projections page, we share a few items about the team's home ballpark. There's the aforementioned diagram of the park's dimensions (including distances to the outfield wall), a few important biographical facts about the stadium, a graphic showing the height of the wall from the left-field pole to the right-field pole, and a table showing three-year park factors for the stadium. The park factors are displayed as indexes where 100 is average, 110 means that the park inflates the statistic in question by 10 percent, and 90 means that the park deflates the statistic in question by 10 percent.

Following the ballpark page, we have a **Personnel** section that lists many of the important decision-makers and upper-level field and operations staff members for the franchise, as well as any former Baseball Prospectus staff members who are currently part of the organization.

Position Players

After all that information and a thoughtful bylined essay covering each team, we present our player comments. Each player is listed with the major-league team who employed him as of early January 2019. If a player changed teams after that point via free agency, trade, or any other method, you'll be able to find them in the book for their previous squad.

First, we cover biographical information (age is as of June 30, 2019) before moving onto the stats themselves. Our statistic columns include standard identifying information like **YEAR**, **TEAM**, **LVL** (level of affiliated play) and **AGE**

Baltimore Orioles 2019

before getting into the numbers. Next, we provide raw, unstranslated numbers like you might find on the back of your dad's baseball cards: **PA** (plate appearances), **R** (runs), **2B** (doubles), **3B** (triples), **HR** (home runs), **RBI** (runs batted in), **BB** (walks), **K** (strikeouts), **SB** (stolen bases) and **CS** (caught stealing). Then we have unadjusted "slash" statistics: **AVG** (batting average), **OBP** (on-base percentage) and **SLG** (slugging percentage).

Just below the stats box is **PECOTA** data, which is discussed further in a following section. After that, it's on to a pithy and always-informative comment written by a member of the Baseball Prospectus staff, before we cover more stats.

The second text box repeats YEAR, TEAM, LVL, AGE, and PA, then moves on to **DRC+** (Deserved Runs Created Plus), which we described earlier as total offensive expected contribution compared to the league average. Next, one of our oldest active metrics, **VORP** (Value Over Replacement Player), considers offensive production, position and plate appearances. In essence, it is the number of runs contributed beyond what a replacement-level player at the same position would contribute if given the same percentage of team plate appearances. VORP does not consider the quality of a player's defense.

BABIP (batting average on balls in play) tells us how often a ball in play fell for a hit, and can help us identify whether a batter may have been lucky or not … but note that high BABIPs also tend to follow the great hitters of our time, as well as speedy singles hitters who put the ball on the ground.

The next item is **BRR** (Baserunning Runs), which covers all of a player's baserunning accomplishments which includes (but isn't limited to) swiped bags and failed attempts. Next is **FRAA** (Fielding Runs Above Average), which also includes the number of games previously played at each position noted in parentheses. Multi-position players have only their two most frequent positions listed here, but their total FRAA number reflects all positions played.

Our last column here is **WARP** (Wins Above Replacement Player). WARP estimates the total value of a player, which means for hitters it takes into account hitting runs above average (calculated using the DRC+ model), BRR and FRAA. Then, it makes an adjustment for positions played and gives the player a credit for plate appearances based upon the difference between "replacement level"¬–which is derived from the quality of players added to a team's roster after the start of the season¬–and the league average.

Catchers

Catchers are a special breed, and thus they have earned their own separate box which displays some of the defensive metrics that we've built just for them. As an example, let's check out J.T. Realmuto.

YEAR	TEAM	P. COUNT	FRM RUNS	BLK RUNS	THRW RUNS	TOT RUNS
2016	MIA	18935	-8.5	1.8	2.1	-5.6
2017	MIA	18959	5.3	1.7	1.0	9.1
2018	MIA	16399	-0.4	0.9	0.1	0.4
2019	PHI	18448	-1.4	1.5	0.7	0.8

The **YEAR** and **TEAM** columns match what you'd find in the other stat box. **P. COUNT** indicates the number of pitches thrown while the catcher was behind the plate, including swinging strikes, fouls, and balls in play. **FRM RUNS** is the total run value the catcher provided (or cost) his team by influencing the umpire to call strikes where other catchers did not. **BLK RUNS** expresses the total run value above or below average for the catcher's ability to prevent wild pitches and passed balls. **THRW RUNS** is calculated using a similar model as the previous two statistics, and it measures a catcher's ability to throw out basestealers but also to dissuade them from testing his arm in the first place. It takes into account factors like the pitcher (including his delivery and pickoff move) and baserunner (who could be as fast as Billy Hamilton or as slow as Yonder Alonso). **TOT RUNS** is the sum of all of the previous three statistics.

Pitchers

Let's give our pitchers a turn, using 2018 NL Cy Young winner Jacob deGrom as our example. Take a look at his first stat block: the first line and the **YEAR**, **TEAM**, **LVL** and **AGE** columns are the same as in the position player example earlier.

Here too, we have a series of columns that display raw, unadjusted statistics compiled by the pitcher over the course of a season: **W** (wins), **L** (losses), **SV** (saves), **G** (games pitched), **GS** (games started), **IP** (innings pitched), **H** (hits allowed) and **HR** (home runs allowed). Next we have two statistics that are rates: **BB/9** (walks per nine innings) and **K/9** (strikeouts per nine innings), before returning to the unadjusted **K** (strikeouts).

Next up is **GB%** (ground ball percentage), which is the percentage of all batted balls that were hit in the ground, including both outs and hits. Remember, this is based on observational data and subject to human error, so please approach this with a healthy dose of skepticism.

BABIP (batting average on balls in play) is calculated using the same methodology as it is for position players, but it often tells us more about a pitcher than it does a hitter. With pitchers, a high BABIP is often due to poor defense or bad luck, and can often be an indicator of potential rebound, and a low BABIP may be cause to expect performance regression. (A typical league-average BABIP is close to .290-.300.)

After a witty 150ish words on the player like only Baseball Prospectus's staff can provide, it's on to that second stat block, which repeats the YEAR, TEAM, LVL, and AGE columns. The metrics **WHIP** (walks plus hits per inning pitched) and **ERA**

Baltimore Orioles 2019

(earned run average) are old standbys: WHIP measures walks and hits allowed on a per-inning basis, while ERA measures earned runs on a nine-inning basis. Neither of these stats are translated or adjusted.

DRA (Deserved Run Average) was described at length earlier, and measures how many runs the pitcher "deserved" to allow per nine innings. Please note that since we lack all the data points that would make for a "real" DRA for minor-league events, the DRA displayed for minor league partial-seasons is based off of different data. (That data is a modified version of our cFIP metric, which you can find more information about on our website.)

Jacob deGrom   RHP
Born: 06/19/88   Age: 31   Bats: L   Throws: R
Height: 6'4"   Weight: 180   Origin: Round 9, 2010 Draft (#272 overall)

YEAR	TEAM	LVL	AGE	W	L	SV	G	GS	IP	H	HR	BB/9	K/9	K	GB%	BABIP
2016	NYN	MLB	28	7	8	0	24	24	148	142	15	2.2	8.7	143	47%	.312
2017	NYN	MLB	29	15	10	0	31	31	201[1]	180	28	2.6	10.7	239	48%	.305
2018	NYN	MLB	30	10	9	0	32	32	217	152	10	1.9	11.2	269	48%	.281
2019	NYN	MLB	31	13	9	0	31	31	186	145	18	2.3	10.7	221	46%	.286

Breakout: 8%   Improve: 29%   Collapse: 28%   Attrition: 6%   MLB: 85%
Comparables: Erik Bedard, A.J. Burnett, CC Sabathia

YEAR	TEAM	LVL	AGE	WHIP	ERA	DRA	WARP	MPH	FB%	WHF	CSP
2016	NYN	MLB	28	1.20	3.04	3.30	3.5	96.3	59.6	12.1	47.2
2017	NYN	MLB	29	1.19	3.53	3.02	5.7	97.2	55.5	14.5	49.5
2018	NYN	MLB	30	0.91	1.70	2.09	8.0	98.2	52.1	16.3	48.4
2019	NYN	MLB	31	1.02	2.91	3.23	3.9	96.6	54.5	14.8	48.2

Just like with hitters, **WARP** (Wins Above Replacement Player) is a total value metric that puts pitchers of all stripes on the same scale as position players. We use DRA as the primary input for our calculation of WARP. You might notice that relief pitchers (due to their limited innings) may have a lower WARP than you were expecting or than you might see in other WARP-like metrics. WARP does not take leverage into account, just the actions a pitcher performs and the expected value of those actions ... which ends up judging high-leverage relief pitchers differently than you might imagine given their prestige and market value.

MPH gives you the pitcher's 95th percentile velocity for the noted season, in order to give you an idea of what the *peak* fastball velocity a pitcher possesses. Since this comes from our pitch tracking data, it is not publicly available for minor-league pitchers.

Finally, we display the three new pitching metrics we described earlier. **FB%** (fastball percentage) gives you the percentage of fastballs thrown out of all pitches. **WhiffRt** (whiff rate) tells you the percentage of swinging strikes induced out of all pitches. **CS Prob** (called strike probability) expresses the likelihood of all pitches thrown to result in a called strike, after controlling for factors like handedness, umpire, pitch type, count, and location.

PECOTA

All players have PECOTA projections for 2019, as well as a set of other numbers that describe the performance of comparable players according to PECOTA. All projections for 2019 are for the player at the date we went to press in early January and are projected into the league and park context as indicated by the team abbreviation. All PECOTA projected statistics represent a player's projected major-league performance.

The numbers beneath the player's stats–Breakout, Improve, Collapse, Attrition–are part and parcel of the PECOTA projections. They estimate the likelihood of changes in performance relative to the player's previously-established level of production, based on the performance of comparable players:

Breakout Rate is the percent change that a player's production will improve by at least 20 percent relative to the weighted average of his performance over his most recent seasons.

Improve Rate is the percent chance that a player's production will improve at all relative to his baseline performance. A player who is expected to perform just the same as he has in the recent past will have an Improve Rate of 50 percent.

Collapse Rate is the percent chance that a position player's production will decline by at least 25 percent relative to his baseline performance.

Attrition Rate operates on playing time rather than performance. Specifically, it measures the likelihood that a player's playing time will decrease by at least 50 percent relative to his established level.

Breakout Rate and Collapse Rate can sometimes be counterintuitive for players who have already experienced a radical change in performance level. It's also worth noting that the projected decline in a player's rate performances might not be indicative of an expected decline in underlying ability or skill, but could just be an anticipated correction following a breakout season.

MLB% is the percentage of similar players who played in the major leagues in their relevant season.

The final pieces of information are the player's three highest-scoring comparable players as determined by PECOTA. All comparables represent a snapshot of how the listed player was performing at the same age as the current player, so if a 23-year-old pitcher is compared to Bartolo Colon, he's actually being compared to a 23-year-old Colon, not the version that pitched for the Rangers in 2018, nor to Colon's career as a whole.

Baltimore Orioles 2019

A few points about pitcher projections. First, we aren't yet projecting peak velocity, so that column will be blank in the PECOTA lines. Second, projecting DRA is trickier than evaluating past performance, because it is unclear how deserving each pitcher will be of his anticipated outcomes. However, we know that another DRA-related statistic–contextual FIP or cFIP–estimates future run scoring very well. So for PECOTA, the projected DRA figures you see are based on the past cFIPs generated by the pitcher and comparable players over time, along with the other factors described above.

Lineouts

In each chapter's Lineouts section, you'll find abbreviated text comments, as well as most of same information you'd find in our full player comments. We limit the stats boxes in this section to only including the 2018 information for each player.

Exclusive Player Visualizations

In our constant battle to provide you with new and interesting baseball content you can't find anywhere else, we've added a trio of data visualizations to each hitter's entry in these books and a pair of visualizations for each pitcher.

For hitters, you'll find three new infographics. The first is each player's **Batted Ball Distribution**, which displays the five major sections of the field: LF (left), LCF (left center), CF (center), RCF (right center), and RF (right). The percentage indicated tells us what percentage of batted balls from that hitter fell within that part of the field during the 2018 season. We've also included the hitter's slugging percentage on balls in play (also called **SLGCON**) for that part of the field.

You'll also see two heatmaps: **Strike Zone vs LHP** and **Strike Zone vs RHP**. These heat maps represent a view of the strike zone from behind the catcher. Areas where there is a darker coloration represent the places where a higher percentage of pitches resulted in hits. In other words, the heatmap represents a hitter's "sweet spots" for getting hits against either left-handed or right-handed pitchers, depending on the image.

Pitchers get two images that help explain what their pitches look like from a hitter's perspective: **Pitch Shape vs LHH** and **Pitch Shape vs RHH**. These images show you the shape and the "tunneling" effect of each pitcher's offerings from the batter's perspective. For each type of pitch that a pitcher throws (represented by an indicator shape), there's a set of dots indicating the flight path, where each dot represents a 0.01-second interval. This maps the average trajectory and speed of an offering, ending where the ball crosses the plate. The solid black box represents the regular strike zone, while the gray contour lines indicate the range of locations that a pitcher typically works in.

Below the image, we provide a bit more detailed information about each pitcher's average offering in the **Pitch Types** box. Here, we also list each of the pitcher's major offerings under the **Type** column.

- **Fastballs** (which usually refers to the four-seam variation)
- **Sinkers** and/or two-seam fastballs
- **Cutters** (which could include "hard" cutters like cut fastballs and "soft" cutters that resemble hard sliders)
- **Changeups** (not including most splitters)
- **Splitters** (split-fingered pitches, forkballs, and some split-changes)
- **Sliders** and/or slurves
- **Curveballs** (including spike-curveballs and knuckle-curveballs, as well as some slurvy curves)
- **Slow curveballs** and/or eephus pitches
- **Knuckleballs**
- **Screwballs**

The **Freq** column indicates the percentage of overall pitches that fall into each of those type categories; if a pitcher has a 16.55% score for changeups, then that's the percent of all pitches that he throws as changeups. **Velo** is exactly what you think it is: the average miles per hour for each pitch type. **H Mov** is the number of inches of horizontal movement on the average pitch of that type, while **V Mov** is the number of inches of vertical movement on the average pitch of that type. (At Baseball Prospectus, we measure this over the long flight of the ball and include gravity into the V Mov number in order to give you the most realistic representation of what the pitch *actually* does.)

If you're wondering about the second number in brackets, that's the index for that velocity or movement compared to the league average. Like DRC+, a score of 100 means that the speed or movement is about the same as league average, while a higher score means that there's higher velocity or movement than the league average. Numbers below 100 indicate less velocity or movement than the league average.

Part 1: Team Analysis

Table for Two: Previewing the 2019 Baltimore Orioles

Darius Austin and Kate Preusser

Studies show that sports fans get a little hit of dopamine to their brains when their team wins. But what about when that team does not take DJ Khaled's advice to win, win, win? What if said team is trapped in a division with two of the sports' perennial powerhouses and another one with roughly 4,396 Top-100 prospects (not to mention a fourth featuring the second coming of Miguel Cabrera)? What if this team is the worst-projected team PECOTA has ever seen, and is flirting dangerously with triple-digit losses for the second straight year? Whence shall these fans get their deserved dose of dopamine? We endeavored to find out.

KATE PREUSSER: Darius, clearly the easiest way for sports fans to get their dopamine fix is from a team that's already in the high cotton, and ideally one that already has a coterie of young stars safely ensconced in its bosom for the foreseeable future. But what of our poor Orioles, who are decidedly not living high on the hog? Is there any hope for a potential breakout from any of the folks who are already there?

DARIUS AUSTIN: There are potentially a lot of young players in this lineup, so if you're trying hard to look for reasons to be optimistic—and I think that's the case for both us and most Orioles fans—then you can hang your hat on that. There's conceivably a starting lineup here where seven of the nine are 26 or younger, and if they can get away from both Mark Trumbo and Chris Davis somehow then the eldest would be 28.

PECOTA thinks Rule 5 pick Richie Martin, Hanser Alberto, Austin Hays and Cedric Mullins are the most likely hitting breakouts. Given where those names are starting from, I'm not sure it's a ringing endorsement, as there still isn't an above-average projection on this team by DRC+, and only Trey Mancini is close at 98. Still, it's something, and Mullins in particular might actually be fun to watch.

KATE: Hanser Alberto was just DFA'd in order to claim lefty Josh Osich off waivers from the Giants, which seems like a bummer to give away one of their hitting breakouts, but [*gestures in direction of the Orioles bullpen*]. Boyce Cedric Mullins II is the Oriole I am most excited to watch, both on and off the field. A fun-sized player selected in the 13th round out of a non-powerhouse college, Mullins has defied expectations as he's zipped through the Orioles' minor leagues, showing speed and surprising pop for someone who stands 5'8". He gets on base, he doesn't strike out, and he plays with schoolyard joy combined with professional poise. Baltimore fans deserve a come-from-nowhere success story, and Mullins could be that story. There's certainly nothing standing in his way to securing the starting center field/leadoff hitter gig, as the team has declined to sign any free agents of note other than *checks notes* Nate Karns, although they did belly up to the table in the Rule 5 draft.

DARIUS: I am quite intrigued by Martin, particularly because a lot of people seemed to be surprised that the A's let him go and he actually seems to have a chance to be a good major leaguer. The team was projected to carry both him and Drew Jackson on the roster all year, at least until they signed Alcides Escobar, which feels like the team trying to teach us a lesson for attempting to be optimistic. As much as I'm interested in Martin, I don't think it says very good things about your lineup when you take two players that other teams didn't really want that much and give them a roster spot all year.

KATE: The A's have a fairly stacked infield and the Dodgers have good players coming out of their ears, so a castoff from those systems might be simply a victim of circumstances. It's possible Drew Jackson is still shaking off the effects of the Stanford Swing, and he's certainly been well-indoctrinated now into the church of Elevation Celebration, although his strikeouts have also elevated. He's the superior defender, as well, so I'd give Jackson the edge, if there is one to be had here. Rule 5 draft picks are a fairly low-risk investment, and if one or both don't work out, they can just move on to someone else.

DARIUS: At the same time, I wonder if there's a certain advantage to the freedom this team has, in the same way that players who have hit rock bottom are open to trying new things. One of the main drivers of dopamine hits in sports is the unexpected. Is that one source of dopamine here—that they are going to try some young guys like Martin who simply have the lure of the unknown? Or are we expecting too much given that they just saw fit to bring Escobar into the fold, a 32-year-old whose OBP hasn't seen the right side of .300 in a half-decade?

KATE: Escobar, even on a minors deal, is… a move, for sure. I think that one is less "lure of the unknown" and more "l'appel du vide", but I agree that this is a particular freedom the Orioles have. I'm not even sure we can yell too much at the Orioles about not going harder in free agency, given the state of ruin in which the organization is currently mired. Their best bet is probably to go after one-year deals for players they can flip at the deadline to help rebuild the farm.

DARIUS: That might work with Karns, who is still something of a projection darling, yet hasn't thrown a major league pitch since May 2017. He's also 31. The fact that he's the best starter by DRA helps to explain why PECOTA projects the Orioles to give up 903 runs, which is 11 more than a 115-loss team just surrendered. That's not so much kicking a team while it's down as repeatedly running it over with a truck and then setting it on fire.

At 26, Dylan Bundy seems like the only hope for a young, reasonably high upside starter. He also gave up 41 homers last year. There isn't a single top-200 pitcher by DRA on this team. Where do you think we find dopamine hits on this pitching staff? Is it when they get out of a jam on a double play?

KATE: The easiest way would be strikeouts, but those will be tough to come by on a team that's projected to be last in baseball in DRA. Last year PECOTA was almost spot-on with its prediction for Alex Cobb (an ERA of 4.92 and a 5.45 DRA); where PECOTA missed was in thinking Cobb would register a positive WARP, as Cobb threw 20+ more innings than PECOTA thought he would. The system predicts a similar performance for 2019, but I think there's a chance Cobb scrapes triple-digit strikeouts this year; his changeup is starting to get whiffs again and is showing more of the depth it did when it was one of the best pitches in baseball. On a pitching staff that's not predicted to earn a ton of strikeouts, hold tight to your Things, even if they are a little careworn.

So if Orioles fans are limited in the joy they can extract from the players on the field–and knowing that any of those player who do succeed will likely find themselves as trade bait at the deadline–what about promises of happier days ahead under new leadership with a bold vision for the future of Birdland?

DARIUS: The front office overhaul seems like it *should* lead to bold, exciting changes, although it's hard to tell exactly what the tangible differences are this early. Mike Elias and Sig Mejdal have just been through one of the most successful rebuilds in recent memory with the Astros and should drastically improve the team's approach in all sorts of areas. We don't really know what Brandon Hyde will be like as manager, but anything new is probably good in this situation. Some fans will probably be more willing to give this new unit far more time than they would have been with the people who put them through 2018. Hope is easier to find here, I think.

KATE: There's always hope in the spring before the games are played, and especially when it's still the honeymoon phase with new leadership. Even with the caveat that a massive Astros-style rebuild isn't feasible today, I think as long as things Feel Different to Orioles fans, they'll be willing to walk fairly far down the garden path with this new leadership. There's been much said about the Orioles getting more involved in international signings, and while that's borne some fruit, other teams like the Marlins have been much more active in snapping up top international players to rebuild their farm system. Baltimore is going to be playing catch-up in that area for a long time.

They're also going to be playing catch-up with analytics: not just culling the underperformers and finding new talent, but also creating an organizational culture that fosters curiosity about and engagement with analytics. While other teams are hiring outside of the traditional ex-player model and instead looking at hitting gurus from the collegiate level and pitching coaches who run their own biomechanics labs, the Orioles have gone fairly traditional with their coaching hires at the major-league level, although they did make some intriguing amateur hires at the minor-league level. That kind of reshaping a culture takes time, though, and is largely done well below the radar of the average fan looking to have a fun night at the ballpark. What will some of the small green shoots of hope look like as the Orioles (hopefully) begin to emerge from the long winter of being an objectively poorly-run baseball organization?

DARIUS: There's something very nebulous about assessing the machinations of a front office. Presumably Mejdal and company are hard at work building an in-house system along the lines of Houston's Ground Control, which will likely inform many decisions in terms of player acquisition and development. If those are the roots we don't get to see, the signs of life might be first evident in those personnel changes, particularly size and composition of the analytics department, but more obvious to the fans will be the types of players they pick up in trade and free agency, as well as how they do it. The days of not only Davis-style contracts but also the type of deal they gave to Cobb last season are gone, and it might be the first Charlie Morton-type acquisition—the kind of low-cost move which proves to be rather more productive than anyone initially conceived—which makes the majority of fans aware that things have changed.

What Elias does with the scouting department will also be telling, although if he takes a similar approach to Luhnow, it might not be a positive change for the scouts themselves. It would also make Orioles fans feel much better if the farm system was ranked considerably better in a year than it is now.

KATE: That's a tall ask for a farm that is regarded in baseball's bottom third with poor international development and not many tradeable assets on the current roster, unless Cobb or Bundy come out strong and the O's are able to to flip them to a pitching-desperate contender. There are some guys worth getting excited about sprinkled around the system–Yusniel Diaz and Ryan Mountcastle, along with Grayson Rodriguez and D.L. Hall (or is he IL Hall now?)–but they're not really all clustered at one level, so beleaguered O's fans don't even have a clear favorite minors team to follow.

If there's nothing compelling on the field to draw fans to the park, the team will need to work extra-hard off the field to fill seats. The "Kids Cheer Free" initiative from last year was a solid start, and season ticket plans are among the most reasonable in MLB (a 13-game plan can run as low as about fifteen bucks a game), but a ballpark pass or other nontraditional ticketing options could cast a wider net. Also, I have done no research on this, but I'm sure the Orioles marketing department has already released a lengthy list of innovative, quality, highly collectible promo items for giveaways this year that has fans chomping at the bit to buy tickets, and they've been teasing out those items for weeks. Now to log on to Orioles dot com for that list…

DARIUS: I personally can't wait for "2019 PROMOTIONS SCHEDULE IS COMING SOON". That's sure to pull in the fans. Wouldn't you think that they'd make this more of a priority given the lack of on-field reasons to come to the park? Some teams have had their schedules out for months. Is this because of the front office turnover? Is Elias locked away somewhere trying to figure out if a David Hess or Stephen Wilkerson bobblehead is going to be the bigger draw?

KATE: Maybe the entire marketing department is buried beneath an avalanche of Andrew Cashner Replica Mullets. Seems like those could go feral pretty easily.

DARIUS: The poor Orioles social media team are at least hard at work trying to promote this team, using the hashtag/knock-off Fanta brand #OrangeSpring. What have they got to work with? Well, there's this Bryce Harper impersonator arriving at Spring Training. It is actually Alex Cobb, but given how many Orioles fans are in the mentions asking a variant of "who?", I feel less bad that we thought this was an attempt to trick the Baltimore faithful into thinking they had actually signed a big name.

There's something rather ominous about Orange Spring, in that it sounds more like the name of a turbulent period of history than a motivational hashtag—the marginally less bloody fall-out of the Red Wedding, perhaps. Some fans already seem to be approaching the season as one of the greatest disasters in sporting history. And even the positive ones are bringing us the dystopian horror of This is Birdland, which… well, Kate, where to start?

KATE: Maybe a miniature Rapsodo machine would be a good ballpark giveaway, as the organization is trying to integrate more advanced technology. Reportedly Dylan Bundy lost track of his pitch count during a bullpen, pointed at the Rapsodo and asked if "that thing" knew how many pitches he'd thrown, which is a story equal parts charming and sad. Again, it really makes #OrangeSpring sound menacing. The analytics bus is coming, and players can either hop on or get run over by it. Now that I think of it, an analytics bus would be a good ballpark giveaway.

Since there is so much up in the air about this team, anything that goes well will be a surprise and a delight. And that's good, because surprises trigger dopamine more than expected positive outcomes. So just know, Orioles fans, that although other fanbases might experience more wins, yours will be all the sweeter.

DARIUS: As cruel as it is to have this team in a division with two of the three best teams in the AL, it does reduce expectations even further and a series win against the Red Sox or Yankees will probably be this season's equivalent of a playoff victory. Maybe that's depressing from one angle, but if you're starting from zero expectations, the dopamine hits are easy to come by.

In addition to unexpected victories generating a bigger dopamine hit, there's also research that suggests that a lot of the benefit of being a fan has nothing to do with winning and losing. Rather, it's about connecting, the bonds fans form with others through their shared identity of supporting the team, and the sense of meaning that gives them. When I was at university, I spent my first year in what was notoriously the worst block on campus—'Cell Block C', as it was dubbed. The bleak breeze-block structure was well past its expiry date. Constructed as temporary accommodation in the 1960s, it was still there 40 years later. People used to say there was no plaster on the corridor walls because it would make them too narrow for fire regulations.

KATE: Wait, breeze-block isn't just an alt-J song?

DARIUS: Faced with the prospect of spending a year in this shoulder-scraping hellhole, a couple of students left fairly quickly. The rest of us bonded over it. We wore the association as a badge of honour: yes, we were from Cell Block C, and we were surviving. We even had t-shirts made. I lived with people from my corridor throughout university, and I remain very good friends with most of them.

I think the 2018-19 Orioles are the Cell Block C of baseball: they're so clearly the worst, they might lose some fans along the way because of it, but most fans are going to band together, keep following, and when they come out the other side they'll have formed stronger, more meaningful bonds than they would have with a mediocre 79-81 season.

KATE: So what you're saying is, the real Birdland is the friends we made along the way? Maybe the Orioles are taking suggestions for that promotional calendar yet. I bet an "I survived the #OrangeSpring" would be a brisk mover. And in that case, I think you're right; the hotter the fire, the stronger the bonds forged there. O's fans are already tempered from last season. If you're going to suck, suck out loud. The O's fans did solid work with #PlayBadlyForAdley; they should devote this season to thinking up rhymes for "Torkelson." 116! 116!

DARIUS: While PECOTA doesn't think it will be that bad, 103 losses is still the worst projection I have ever seen from the system. Starting from the premise that it will be bad, we've probably established that it doesn't really matter *how* bad—with possibly the caveat that being the first team in history to lose 121 games might have some extra negative impact on morale and engagement for all concerned. Is it weird that I want to be 'optimistic' and only predict 99 losses now?

KATE: Yes. It's weird. Cell Block C has warped your brain. Being sad adds to your allostatic load, the things your body needs to do to stay healthy. Being a 2018 Oriole literally made Chance Sisco sick. 99 losses or 105 losses or 116 losses, they're all bad records, Darryl. The best approach for O's fans (and players) is to divest themselves entirely from win-loss records and approach games with a growth mindset and the assurance that the 2019 Orioles, at least, won't cause any cardiac events in the fanbase. In Vegas, Caesar's has the Orioles at 59 wins. Do you take the over or the under?

DARIUS: I'm taking the over, but I'll only go to 60, lest anyone accuse me of being too optimistic. You?

KATE: While a large part of what I love about baseball is its unpredictability, it's too hard for me to look at this team and see more than the occasional bright spot in a relentlessly cloudy sky. Whatever the opposite of the "upgrade" meme is, that's having Manny Machado one year and *uhhh Alcides Escobar, maybe?* the next. Things will get better in Birdland, but I don't know if they're totally at rock-bottom yet. I take the under, emphatically.

Performance Graphs

2018 Hit List Ranking

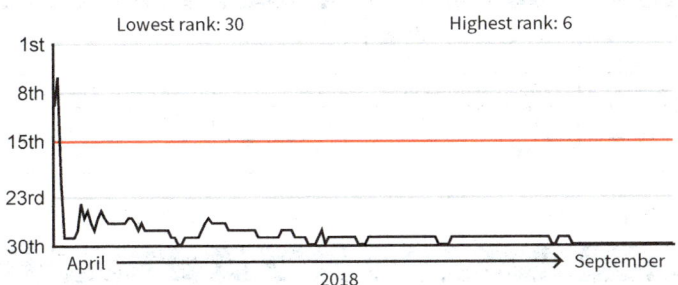

Committed Payroll (in millions)

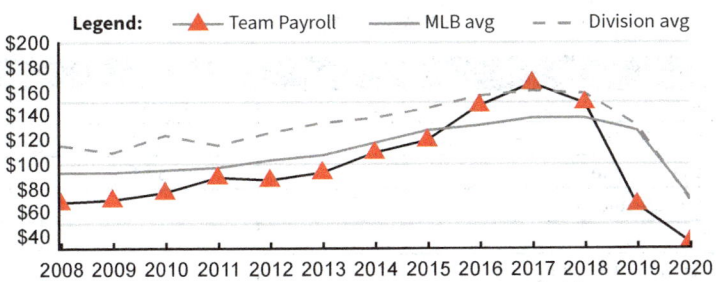

Farm System Ranking

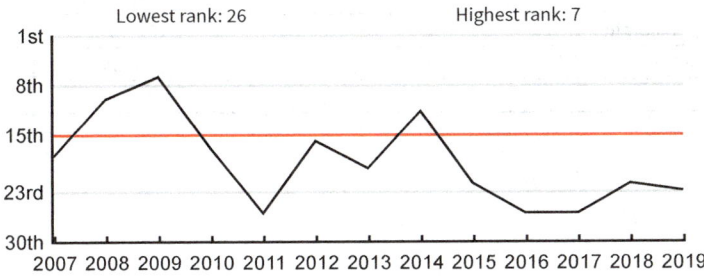

2018 Team Performance

ACTUAL STANDINGS

Team	W	L	Pct
BOS	108	54	.666
NYA	100	62	.617
TBA	90	72	.555
TOR	73	89	.450
BAL	**47**	**115**	**.290**

THIRD-ORDER STANDINGS

Team	W	L	Pct
NYA	99	63	.611
BOS	99	63	.611
TBA	98	64	.604
TOR	70	92	.432
BAL	**54**	**108**	**.333**

TOP HITTERS

Player	WARP
Manny Machado	2.8
Trey Mancini	1.5
Adam Jones	1

TOP PITCHERS

Player	WARP
Kevin Gausman	1.5
Tanner Scott	1.3
Brad Brach	0.4

VITAL STATISTICS

Statistic Name	Value	Rank
Pythagenpat	.335	30th
Runs Scored per Game	3.84	27th
Runs Allowed per Game	5.51	30th
Deserved Runs Created Plus	88	27th
Deserved Run Average	5.88	29th
Fielding Independent Pitching	5.01	30th
Defensive Efficiency Rating	.690	30th
Batter Age	28.4	20th
Pitcher Age	27.0	6th
Salary	$148.6M	13th
Marginal $ per Marginal Win	$100.0M	1st
Disabled List Days	$1,248.0M	16th
$ on DL	19%	20th

2019 Team Projections

PROJECTED STANDINGS

Team	W	L	Pct	+/-
NYA	96	66	.592	-4
BOS	90	72	.555	-18
TBA	85	77	.524	-5
TOR	76	86	.469	+3
BAL	**57**	**105**	**.351**	**+10**

TOP PROJECTED HITTERS

Player	WARP
Trey Mancini	1.4
Jonathan Villar	1.1
Cedric Mullins	1.1

TOP PROJECTED PITCHERS

Player	WARP
Dylan Bundy	1.9
Dean Kremer	1.5
Zac Lowther	1.0

FARM SYSTEM REPORT

Top Prospect	Number of Top 101 Prospects
Yusniel Diaz, #44	3

KEY DEDUCTIONS

Player	WARP
Adam Jones	2
Breyvic Valera	0.4

KEY ADDITIONS

Player	WARP

Team Personnel

Executive Vice President, General Manager
Mike Elias

Assistant General Manager, Analytics
Sig Mejdal

Manager
Brandon Hyde

Oriole Park at Camden Yards Stats

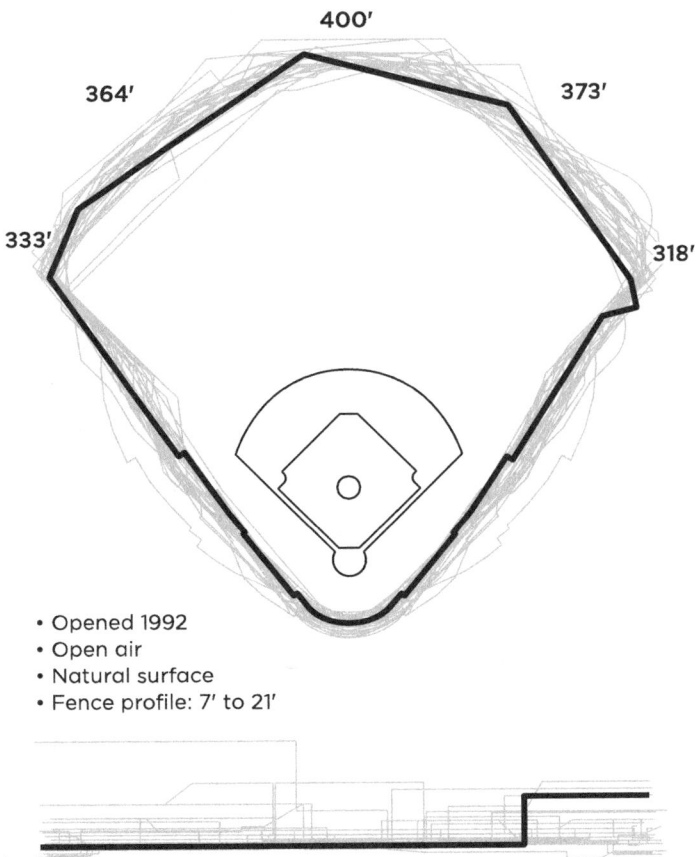

- Opened 1992
- Open air
- Natural surface
- Fence profile: 7' to 21'

Three-Year Park Factors

Runs	Runs/RH	Runs/LH	HR/RH	HR/LH
99	100	98	107	103

Orioles Team Analysis

A clean break with the past can be a good thing. For a baseball franchise with a history of being a punching bag and a punchline, it should be the most important thing. But for the Baltimore Orioles, it might be fairly considered to be the only thing they had left.

Buck Showalter is gone. Dan Duquette is gone. Manny Machado, Jonathan Schoop, Zach Britton, Adam Jones, all of them are gone. Darren O'Day, Brad Brach, Kevin Gausman will be absent as well. The senior-ranking member of the 2019 Baltimore Orioles with any heavy association with the teams that went to the playoffs three times, won the American League East once, and finished in last place the past two seasons will be Dylan Bundy, and it's probably just a matter of time for him, too. The future is bright, and blindingly uncertain.

There have been a lot of words written about new general manager and executive vice president of baseball operations, Mike Elias, and his new field manager, Brandon Hyde; there's no need to repeat them here in full, but Elias was one of Jeff Luhnow's few seconds atop the Houston Astros front office during their rise through the American League, and Hyde served as bench coach and first base coach during the ascension of the Chicago Cubs before joining Baltimore. The Cubs won the Series in 2016; the Astros won it in 2017. Each franchise is seen as the class of its respective league in both process and results. If you wanted a series of hires to wipe away all doubts that the Orioles were joining the modern age, you quite literally could not have scripted them better than this. Elias even brought over Sig Mejdal, the analytics genius who turned Houston's program around. You might not have heard, but he used to work for NASA. The previous head of analytics for the Orioles, Sarah Gelles, has left for a new job with...the Houston Astros. Perhaps the issue before with Baltimore's analytics before wasn't the ideas, but the implementation—either way, Elias has an excellent history of ensuring that implementation.

Indeed, one of Elias's first and strongest promises was to overhaul the way the Orioles do business on a fundamental level, and unlike his predecessor, he was given the authority to clean house immediately. He's spent the offseason molding the Warehouse on Eutaw Street into the sort of machine that Houston used to achieve their championship with maximum efficiency, and he will attend to that machine with a watchmaker's eye. Hyde will be his man on the field level, his most important work being done outside of the box scores and perhaps even outside of the season itself, developing raw players in spring training and then polishing the few of them that make his active roster in the majors. Baltimore will seize every advantage, exploit every rule, and take every inch they are given by rule and by law to make themselves into a lean, competitive organization; that is what the Angelos family is paying for, and as the conventional wisdom goes, that is what a club needs to do if they're sharing a division with the Red Sox and Yankees.

Baltimore will finally join the rest of the league in a healthy pursuit of teenagers from the global south via international free agency. They will hopefully avoid the pratfalls and outright criminal acts that have led to the Atlanta Braves getting a general manager banned from baseball for life, or to an FBI investigation into the Los Angeles Dodgers revealing a spreadsheet ranking overseas contractors by level of suspected criminality. The international market for amateur players is one of the few remaining true free markets in baseball, with all of the lawlessness that implies; Major League Baseball is thankfully getting that under control by degrees, the posting agreement with the Cuban league being the latest step in making sure players don't have to turn to human traffickers to get to America and play ball. If there's any time to be joining, it's now—but, at least in the past, perhaps this was one area that patriarch Peter Angelos was right to stay away from, even if it did hurt the team on the field. The Orioles have their slot money, however, and there's no sense in them not using it. One has to assume the new regime will find a better use to which to put it than mediocre relievers at the trade deadline.

The watchwords of the modern MLB team are "financial flexibility," and the good news for the incoming regime is they have it by...the truckload? By whatever means you judge a concept which embodies not action, but being in a state in which you could act. Elias entered the winter with three contracts worth over $10 million annually on his books, and only one of them—you know which one—being of such ludicrous negative value that it will remain there for at least another season or two. Alex Cobb and Mark Trumbo are both useful major league pieces with the chance to flash much, much brighter given the right run of luck and health, and even if Baltimore can't move them at the deadline, they're looking at a roster commitment of some $65 to $70 million for 2019. That's half (or less so, more likely) the player payroll for 2018. That's incredible financial flexibility...and it would be silly to use it on free agents on a team in the middle of a tear-down, so presumably those savings will be put back into the organization in the form of player development and facilities upgrades, rather than merely being pocketed. That's what the Los Angeles Dodgers did—not Elias's Astros or Hyde's Cubs, but the Dodgers—and it has paid dividends for them, even if it hasn't gotten them a ring yet.

The casual fan will likely know only a few of the players on Baltimore's Opening Day roster next season, but that's just an opportunity to grow to care about a whole host of brand new faces. The good ones will get traded away, of course, and the important ones won't show up until May or June. Even if your new favorite player makes it through the year on the active roster, that just makes it more likely he'll be dealt before spring rolls around, as teams have gravitated strongly away from the deadline and towards November for impact trades over the past few seasons. But the odds say that at least one or two of the guys on the field for the anthem the first time around next year will be on the next decent Orioles team. The odds point heavily towards one, however. Probably a catcher.

There is one unalloyed bit of good news: paying attention to Baltimore's minor league system will no longer be the exercise in masochism it was for...well, likely for as long as you can remember. The Orioles still don't have a good system, per se—it lacks credible superstar-grade talent at the top, and real depth at the bottom—but one or two more seasons should fix that, and for now, you can still pay attention to top prospect outfielder Yusniel Diaz as he works on his defense for the first couple months of the season, track Ryan Mountcastle as he figures out whether his position moving forward is left field or first base, and transfer all your dreams into the person of Dillon Tate, because the idea of a pitcher the Yankees traded to the Orioles becoming an ace for Baltimore would be something akin to riding into Camden Yards bearing the Holy Grail.

If you've detected a marked lack of enthusiasm for all this and instead the creeping hold of resignation, well, modern, efficient, maximally-impactful smart baseball is a whole lot more fun to think about than to watch during the first two or three years of the contention cycle. Both the Astros and the Cubs had to stress to fans through sustained PR campaigns that they were going to be bad for a while to be good—and now that both teams have held up their end of the bargain, many other fan bases are eager to sign on without the soft sell. They're not particularly wrong to do so, given the systemic rewards for accumulating cost-controlled young talent, but the first two seasons are brutal. Luhnow's Astros lost 107 and 111 games his first two years at the helm; Epstein's Cubs, 101 and 96. Baltimore lost 115 games last year, which has some fans thinking, "that wasn't so bad; I can do that again."

Perhaps so; history has allowed for braver acts. But you'll have to get through the first half of the season not just without Manny Machado or Kevin Gausman or Jonathan Schoop or any of the bullpen guys, but without something far more important: hope. It was easy to say you saw this all coming last September as the team blew past 100 losses on its way towards the cliff, looking out into that great big sky. In April and May, though, you were telling yourself and everyone who would listen that this team was one solid winning streak from turning things around; that Kevin Gausman was *this* close to figuring it out; that if they had a good year, the team could get Schoop to sign an extension; that if things broke right, maybe Showalter and his managerial magic could all drag this rattling train one more stop down the line.

Baltimore Orioles 2019

Even if you suspected the wheels were about to come off and the engineer had jumped out a dozen mile markers back, there was always the possibility that the bridge wasn't actually out. The Orioles didn't look like a great team going into 2018, but they didn't look like a great team going into 2012 and 2015; what they did look like was a team that was trying to win, even if it didn't all line up on paper. As an Orioles fan going into those seasons, you knew that just because the Orioles shouldn't be a good team didn't mean they couldn't be. That's hope; it might be stupid, it might be overrated, and it certainly isn't compatible with a five-year plan, but it's absolutely necessary if you're going to watch 162 games of Major League Baseball in one calendar year. Few teams have provided that feeling this decade than the logic and PECOTA-defying Baltimore Orioles.

But you cannot have hope in 2019. All you are permitted is Chris Davis.

—Jonathan Bernhardt is an author of The Athletic.

Part 2: Player Analysis

Chris Davis 1B

Born: 03/17/86 Age: 33 Bats: L Throws: R
Height: 6'3" Weight: 230 Origin: Round 5, 2006 Draft (#148 overall)

YEAR	TEAM	LVL	AGE	PA	R	2B	3B	HR	RBI	BB	K	SB	CS	AVG/OBP/SLG
2016	BAL	MLB	30	665	99	21	0	38	84	88	219	1	0	.221/.332/.459
2017	BAL	MLB	31	524	65	15	1	26	61	61	195	1	1	.215/.309/.423
2018	BAL	MLB	32	522	40	12	0	16	49	41	192	2	0	.168/.243/.296
2019	BAL	MLB	33	530	59	19	1	20	65	54	178	1	1	.214/.300/.387

Breakout: 2%   Improve: 15%   Collapse: 19%   Attrition: 14%   MLB: 86%
Comparables: Richie Sexson, Brandon Moss, Mo Vaughn

While most US schoolchildren learn about the Great Chicago Fire, little attention is paid to a much larger fire that occurred on the same day in 1871: the Peshtigo Fire in Wisconsin burned over a million acres of forest and killed scores more than in Chicago, its conditions so deadly that in WWII, US and British soldiers studied the so-called Peshtigo Paradigm to plan bombing campaigns against Axis strongholds. It remains to this day the deadliest wildfire in American history, and yet few outside of the region know about it. This is to say, historical memory is often a social construct, or so Chris Davis should hope it is. This may be the only way to leave the smoking ruin of his historically awful 2018 campaign behind, hoping that somewhere out there in baseball is the equivalent of Mrs. O'Leary's cow and one very tippy lantern.

YEAR	TEAM	LVL	AGE	PA	DRC+	VORP	BABIP	BRR	FRAA	WARP
2016	BAL	MLB	30	665	114	14.6	.279	0.3	1B(152): 5.7, RF(3): -0.1	2.6
2017	BAL	MLB	31	524	88	-2.0	.301	-2.0	1B(125): 4.2, 3B(2): -0.1	0.2
2018	BAL	MLB	32	522	56	-28.5	.237	-4.6	1B(116): -5.4	-3.2
2019	BAL	MLB	33	530	84	-1.2	.293	-0.9	1B -2	-0.3

Chris Davis, continued

Batted Ball Distribution

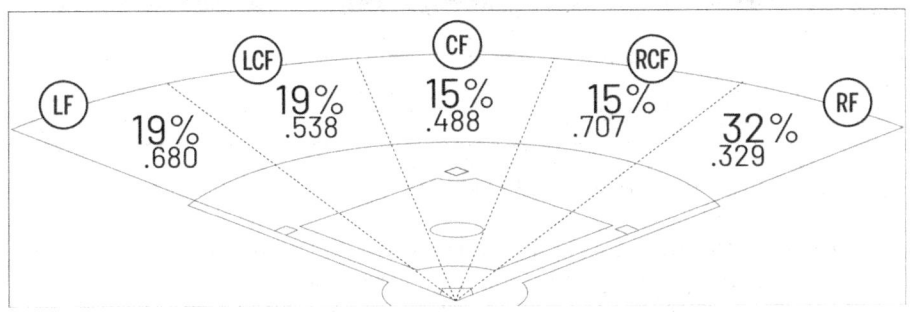

Strike Zone vs LHP **Strike Zone vs RHP**

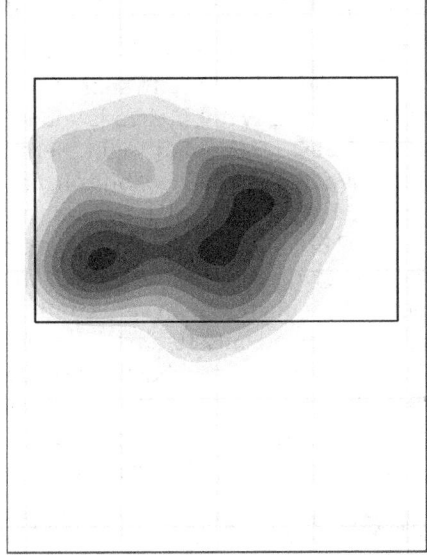

Baltimore Orioles 2019

Alcides Escobar SS

Born: 12/16/86 Age: 32 Bats: R Throws: R
Height: 6'1" Weight: 205 Origin: International Free Agent, 2003

YEAR	TEAM	LVL	AGE	PA	R	2B	3B	HR	RBI	BB	K	SB	CS	AVG/OBP/SLG
2016	KCA	MLB	29	682	57	24	6	7	55	27	96	17	4	.261/.292/.350
2017	KCA	MLB	30	629	71	36	5	6	54	15	102	4	7	.250/.272/.357
2018	KCA	MLB	31	531	54	22	3	4	34	29	74	8	2	.231/.279/.313
2019	BAL	MLB	32	152	15	7	1	2	13	8	23	2	1	.250/.293/.357

Breakout: 4%   Improve: 45%   Collapse: 7%   Attrition: 21%   MLB: 91%
Comparables: Bill Russell, Jimmy Cooney, Bob Lillis

INT. GENERAL MANAGER'S OFFICE. KAUFFMAN STADIUM. As we pan across the room, we see family photographs, framed awards, memorabilia. The camera lingers on a team photo, emblazoned with the legend: "2015 World Champions." We settle on a side view of DAYTON MOORE, well-tanned, middle-aged, wearing a blue polo shirt and sporting a tidy crew cut. As he picks up the office phone, the electronic desk calendar shows a monthly view: "January 2018." Moore's face brightens as he hears a voice on the other end of the line.

"Ned! Hey, it's Dayton. Yeah…you know I don't like texting. Old school, I guess, ha ha. Besides, I wanted to share some good news directly. Yup. So, hey, I got a box of those Esky bobbleheads you asked for… $350 on eBay, would you believe? Says 'Esky Magic' right there on the base. I was the only bidder, but they have this 'Buy It Now' button, and I figured why wait, right?…What?…What?…I don't underst— Oh. Ohhhh. You wanted *literally Alcides Escobar*? But you said 'good luck charm,' and I figured…OK, Ned, hold on…Yeah, I've got a, what you call 'em, one of them 'quants' here…Yeah, I'm being told that Alcides has, uh, not been very good. A .272 on-base percenta—Ned, stop yelling—walked only 15 times *all season*. I know, but I thought we'd try to get Mondesi in there, see what we've got going forward. Yes, of course I remember 2015. Yes, magic, I know. Ned, stop yelling…OK. OK. Yes, I'll call—or text. Yes, right now…Oh, Ned? One more thing. Looks like I'm out $350, so if your next per diem is a little light, it's becau—Ned? Ned?"

YEAR	TEAM	LVL	AGE	PA	DRC+	VORP	BABIP	BRR	FRAA	WARP
2016	KCA	MLB	29	682	76	5.8	.295	0.4	SS(162): 0.8	1.2
2017	KCA	MLB	30	629	71	3.1	.291	0.6	SS(162): 10.0	1.6
2018	KCA	MLB	31	531	74	-1.3	.263	0.0	SS(104): -10.3, 3B(29): 1.3	-0.4
2019	BAL	MLB	32	152	76	1.7	.280	0.0	SS 0	0.1

Alcides Escobar, continued

Batted Ball Distribution

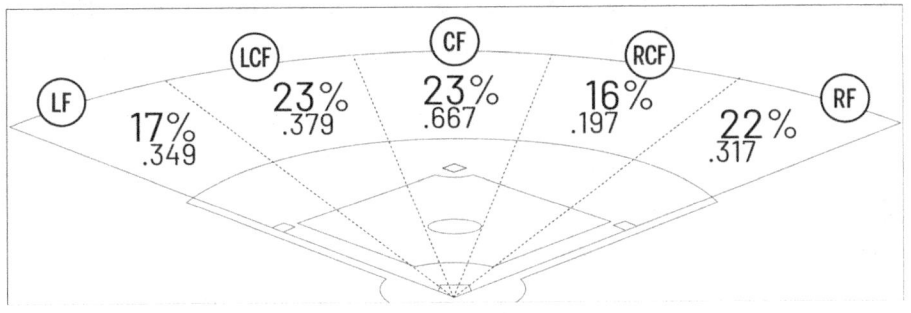

Strike Zone vs LHP **Strike Zone vs RHP**

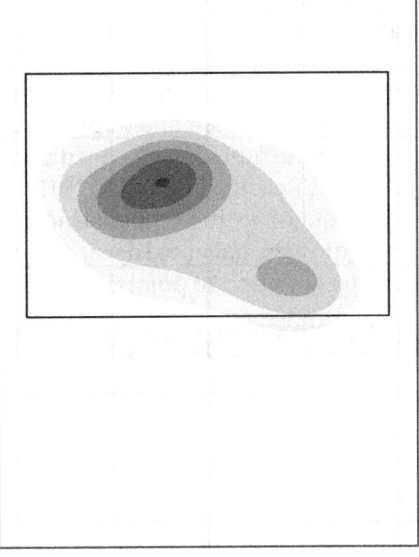

Baltimore Orioles 2019

Trey Mancini LF
Born: 03/18/92   Age: 27   Bats: R   Throws: R
Height: 6'4"   Weight: 215   Origin: Round 8, 2013 Draft (#249 overall)

YEAR	TEAM	LVL	AGE	PA	R	2B	3B	HR	RBI	BB	K	SB	CS	AVG/OBP/SLG
2016	BOW	AA	24	75	18	4	0	7	14	10	17	0	0	.302/.413/.698
2016	NOR	AAA	24	536	60	22	5	13	54	48	123	2	2	.280/.349/.427
2016	BAL	MLB	24	15	3	1	0	3	5	0	4	0	0	.357/.400/1.071
2017	BAL	MLB	25	586	65	26	4	24	78	33	139	1	0	.293/.338/.488
2018	BAL	MLB	26	636	69	23	3	24	58	44	153	0	1	.242/.299/.416
2019	BAL	MLB	27	622	77	24	3	21	69	46	147	1	0	.253/.314/.417

Breakout: 8%   Improve: 45%   Collapse: 17%   Attrition: 12%   MLB: 92%
Comparables: Brennan Boesch, J.D. Martinez, Cody Asche

The greatest irony of Alanis Morissette's 1996 song "Ironic" is that none of the situations described therein are actually ironic, but instead just variations of spectacularly bad luck. That the 2018 Orioles paid Chris Davis and Mark Trumbo over 30 million dollars combined to do nothing other than hit home runs, and the fact that both of them were out-homered by Mancini, is a little bad luck, a lot of poor resource allocation, and significantly more ironic than a black fly in one's chardonnay. In order to manufacture playing time for the team leader in HRs, the O's wedged Mancini—who, of all the first basemen in the world, is the first-basiest—into left and hoped an aging Adam Jones could cover a little extra ground in the outfield, which led to predictably disastrous results (Predictably Disastrous Results: title of the 2018 Orioles' sextape). Perhaps a second year of playing out of position fueled Mancini's brutal first-half slump, but by August he was getting the ball into the air again and doing damage; his second-half slugging jumped 120 points.

YEAR	TEAM	LVL	AGE	PA	DRC+	VORP	BABIP	BRR	FRAA	WARP
2016	BOW	AA	24	75	170	7.8	.308	0.6	1B(15): 0.4	0.6
2016	NOR	AAA	24	536	129	15.4	.351	-1.9	1B(121): 6.5	2.1
2016	BAL	MLB	24	15	120	2.7	.286	-0.1		0.0
2017	BAL	MLB	25	586	106	21.8	.352	0.9	LF(88): 0.9, 1B(45): -2.1	1.6
2018	BAL	MLB	26	636	92	3.0	.285	0.5	LF(98): 4.5, 1B(47): 2.7	1.5
2019	BAL	MLB	27	622	97	13.9	.304	-0.9	LF 1, 1B 1	1.4

Trey Mancini, continued

Batted Ball Distribution

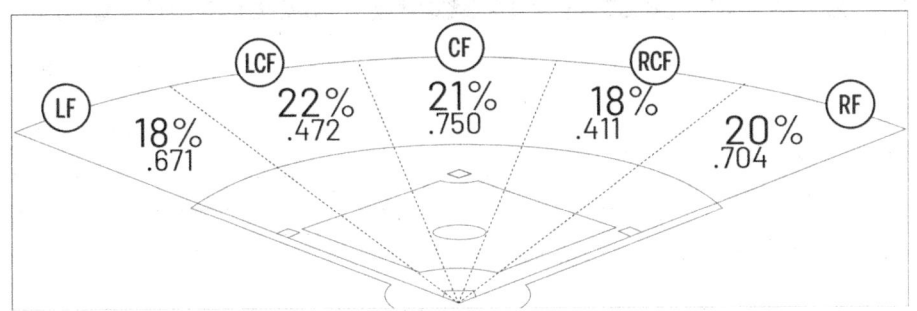

Strike Zone vs LHP

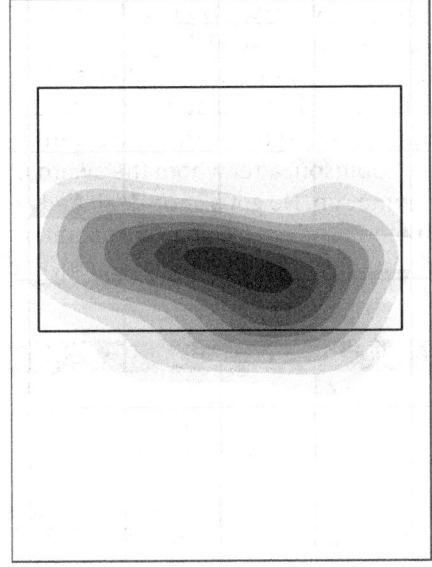

Strike Zone vs RHP

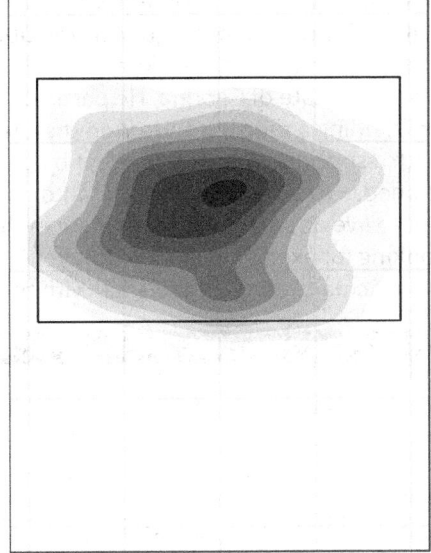

Cedric Mullins CF

Born: 10/01/94 Age: 24 Bats: B Throws: L
Height: 5'8" Weight: 175 Origin: Round 13, 2015 Draft (#403 overall)

YEAR	TEAM	LVL	AGE	PA	R	2B	3B	HR	RBI	BB	K	SB	CS	AVG/OBP/SLG
2016	DEL	A	21	559	79	37	10	14	55	37	101	30	6	.273/.321/.464
2017	BOW	AA	22	350	53	19	1	13	37	27	58	9	7	.265/.319/.460
2018	BOW	AA	23	218	36	12	5	6	28	15	28	9	1	.313/.362/.512
2018	NOR	AAA	23	269	41	17	3	6	19	22	39	12	0	.269/.333/.438
2018	BAL	MLB	23	191	23	9	0	4	11	17	37	2	3	.235/.312/.359
2019	BAL	MLB	24	608	77	28	3	17	59	45	113	14	5	.235/.298/.389

Breakout: 15% Improve: 47% Collapse: 5% Attrition: 27% MLB: 62%
Comparables: Raimel Tapia, Felix Pie, Franklin Gutierrez

Mullins might have been the happiest player on a 108-loss team ever. After tearing up Double-A for the first couple months of the season, Baltimore promoted Mullins to Triple-A on June 1st. There he might have languished if not for Adam Jones, who willingly moved to left to accommodate Mullins, who has plus speed and a flair for dramatic diving catches. And Mullins made the most out of his brief major league tenure: During Player's Weekend, he got to wear a jersey with his chosen nickname ("The Entertainer") and custom kicks depicting his home state of Georgia. He participated in rookie dress-up day (costume: a child riding a dinosaur). He won the Orioles' Minor Leaguer of the Year award, with a special acknowledgement by Brooks Robinson, after whom the award is named. He robbed Giancarlo Stanton of a home run. He got a shoe deal. And he got to live out his dream of playing in the majors, and for a fanbase desperately looking for exactly the kind of player Cedric Mullins is: talented, young, fun, and contractually obligated to stick with them.

YEAR	TEAM	LVL	AGE	PA	DRC+	VORP	BABIP	BRR	FRAA	WARP
2016	DEL	A	21	559	126	39.8	.314	2.2	CF(122): 5.0	3.0
2017	BOW	AA	22	350	100	15.7	.283	0.9	CF(57): 7.2, LF(8): 1.1	1.2
2018	BOW	AA	23	218	135	22.8	.339	2.4	CF(43): 0.4, LF(3): 0.5	1.5
2018	NOR	AAA	23	269	118	15.0	.298	2.2	CF(60): 0.2	1.3
2018	BAL	MLB	23	191	82	1.7	.279	-0.6	CF(45): -3.8, LF(1): 0.0	-0.2
2019	BAL	MLB	24	608	82	12.1	.261	0.9	CF 0	1.1

Cedric Mullins, continued

Batted Ball Distribution

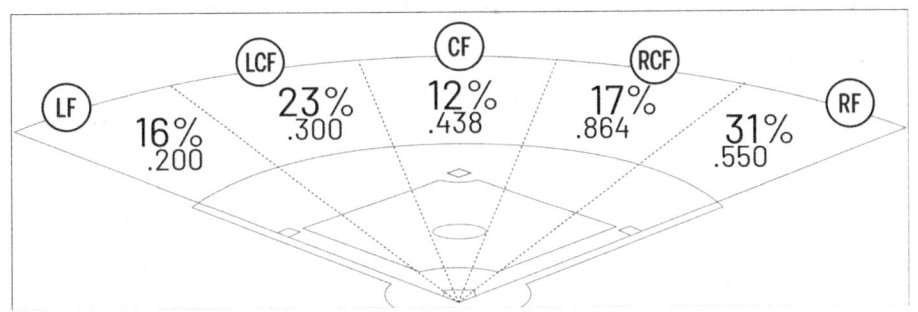

Strike Zone vs LHP

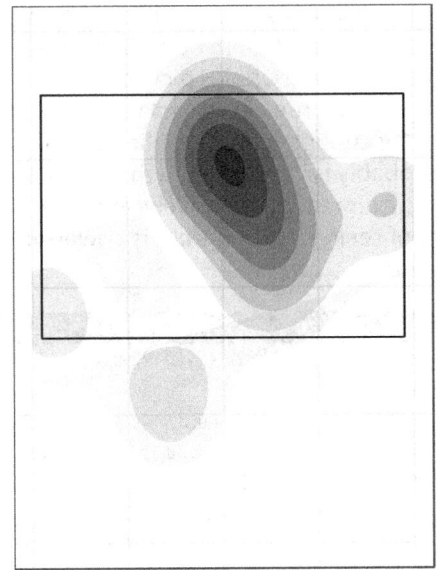

Strike Zone vs RHP

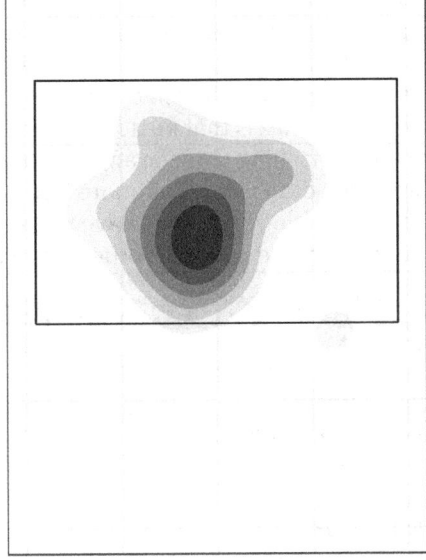

Renato Nunez 3B

Born: 04/04/94 Age: 25 Bats: R Throws: R
Height: 6'1" Weight: 220 Origin: International Free Agent, 2010

YEAR	TEAM	LVL	AGE	PA	R	2B	3B	HR	RBI	BB	K	SB	CS	AVG/OBP/SLG
2016	NAS	AAA	22	550	61	20	2	23	75	31	119	2	0	.228/.278/.412
2016	OAK	MLB	22	15	0	0	0	0	1	0	3	0	0	.133/.133/.133
2017	NAS	AAA	23	533	74	27	2	32	78	47	141	2	1	.249/.319/.518
2017	OAK	MLB	23	16	1	0	0	1	3	1	8	0	0	.200/.250/.400
2018	NAS	AAA	24	30	3	0	0	0	4	2	6	0	0	.357/.400/.357
2018	TEX	MLB	24	41	2	1	0	1	2	3	12	0	0	.167/.244/.278
2018	NOR	AAA	24	228	25	14	1	5	25	23	49	1	0	.289/.361/.443
2018	BAL	MLB	24	220	26	13	0	7	20	16	50	0	0	.275/.336/.445
2019	BAL	MLB	25	444	51	17	1	22	60	25	115	0	0	.214/.264/.420

Breakout: 12%   Improve: 36%   Collapse: 11%   Attrition: 38%   MLB: 74%
Comparables: Brandon Wood, Josh Bell, Mat Gamel

A prospect blocked at all his positions by various Matts and Marks, the A's tried to sneak Nunez through waivers while he was rehabbing a hamstring injury in Triple-A Nashville. He was claimed first by the Rangers before being DFA'd for Rougned Odor's return from the DL, at which point the Orioles picked him up, fixed him up a little bed in the garage, and gave him run of the backyard. The knock on Nunez is that he doesn't have strong enough plate discipline when he's not smashing dingers, and his glove probably isn't good enough to stick at third. That didn't stop Baltimore from playing him there exclusively, and as a non-contending team they have the luxury of seeing if Nunez's bat is powerful enough to make up for his other shortcomings.

YEAR	TEAM	LVL	AGE	PA	DRC+	VORP	BABIP	BRR	FRAA	WARP
2016	NAS	AAA	22	550	87	16.8	.249	0.9	3B(89): -1.2, LF(12): -0.5	-0.1
2016	OAK	MLB	22	15	75	-3.1	.167	-0.7		-0.1
2017	NAS	AAA	23	533	115	24.6	.279	-1.5	LF(48): -7.0, 3B(44): -4.7	0.3
2017	OAK	MLB	23	16	70	-0.5	.333	-0.2	LF(3): -0.2, 3B(1): 0.2	0.0
2018	NAS	AAA	24	30	104	1.4	.455	-0.5	3B(2): -0.2, LF(2): -0.5	0.0
2018	TEX	MLB	24	41	94	-0.7	.208	-0.2	3B(8): 0.9, LF(4): -0.2	0.2
2018	NOR	AAA	24	228	130	12.2	.356	0.8	3B(38): 0.1, 1B(6): 0.6	1.2
2018	BAL	MLB	24	220	95	8.6	.333	-0.8	3B(59): -4.0	0.2
2019	BAL	MLB	25	444	83	0.4	.240	-0.7	3B -4	-0.4

Renato Nunez, continued

Batted Ball Distribution

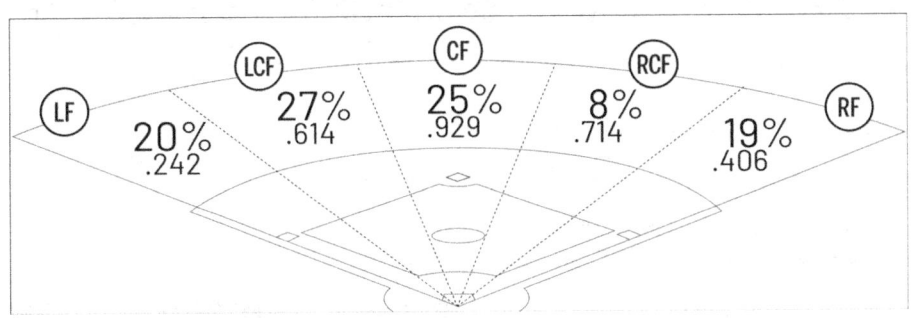

Strike Zone vs LHP

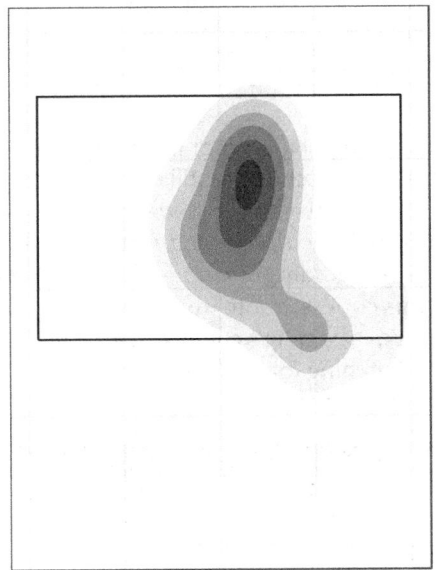

Strike Zone vs RHP

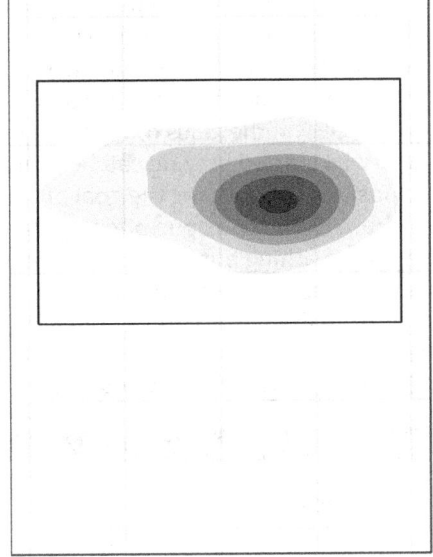

Chance Sisco C

Born: 02/24/95   Age: 24   Bats: L   Throws: R
Height: 6'2"   Weight: 195   Origin: Round 2, 2013 Draft (#61 overall)

YEAR	TEAM	LVL	AGE	PA	R	2B	3B	HR	RBI	BB	K	SB	CS	AVG/OBP/SLG
2016	BOW	AA	21	479	53	28	1	4	44	59	83	2	2	.320/.406/.422
2017	NOR	AAA	22	388	47	23	0	7	47	32	99	2	2	.267/.340/.395
2017	BAL	MLB	22	22	3	2	0	2	4	3	7	0	0	.333/.455/.778
2018	NOR	AAA	23	151	22	5	0	3	12	16	36	0	0	.242/.344/.352
2018	BAL	MLB	23	184	13	8	0	2	16	13	66	1	0	.181/.288/.269
2019	BAL	MLB	24	235	24	11	1	6	24	17	66	0	0	.232/.302/.379

Breakout: 13%   Improve: 34%   Collapse: 0%   Attrition: 26%   MLB: 61%
Comparables: Chris Iannetta, Hank Conger, Josh Donaldson

The Orioles treated Sisco like a trip to a mid-priced buffet this season, giving him a spot on the 25-man out of spring training, only to pile up trips between levels like salad bar-sticky plates. Sisco did strike out his share over the first two months of the season, but also showed off the discerning eye that's kept his OBP in the .330s or higher in every season of his minor league career. Sisco, who started playing catcher only late in high school, is still developing at the position, so perhaps the goal of shifting him between levels was to give him exposure to major-league pitching staffs without becoming overly fatigued by the fire-breathing but poor-commanding arms parading from the O's bullpen on a nightly basis. It's a notion supported by this curious quote from Buck Showalter after Sisco was optioned down: "I'm afraid he's coming down with...He hasn't slept in two or three days." Catching for the 2018 Baltimore Orioles pitching staff: literally a hazard to one's health.

YEAR	TEAM	P. COUNT	FRM RUNS	BLK RUNS	THRW RUNS	TOT RUNS
2017	BAL	653	-0.6	-0.2	-0.1	-1.1
2017	NOR	13196	5.9	1.1	-1.7	4.6
2018	BAL	6491	-2.2	0.3	-0.1	-2.1
2018	NOR	5151	-1.3	0.0	-0.8	-2.0
2019	BAL	8887	-3.3	0.3	-0.8	-3.9

YEAR	TEAM	LVL	AGE	PA	DRC+	VORP	BABIP	BRR	FRAA	WARP
2016	BOW	AA	21	479	148	28.8	.387	-5.7	C(83): -9.8	1.6
2017	NOR	AAA	22	388	115	22.5	.351	1.9	C(94): 3.2	2.5
2017	BAL	MLB	22	22	94	3.9	.444	-0.3	C(10): -0.7	0.0
2018	NOR	AAA	23	151	112	5.4	.308	-1.1	C(37): -2.8	0.3
2018	BAL	MLB	23	184	58	-3.5	.293	-1.3	C(55): -2.8	-0.5
2019	BAL	MLB	24	235	82	5.1	.299	-0.5	C -6	-0.2

Chance Sisco, continued

Batted Ball Distribution

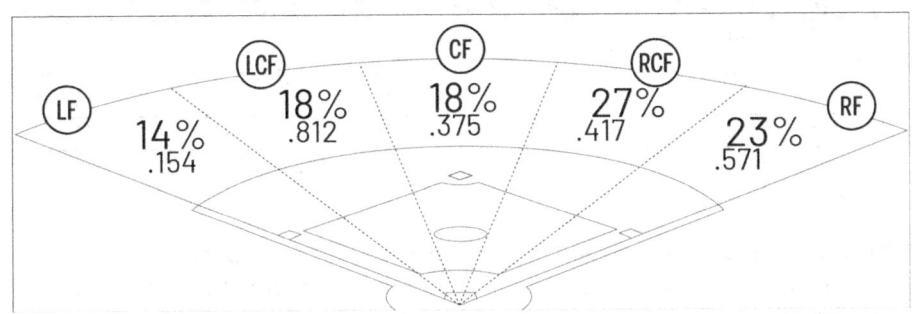

Strike Zone vs LHP   **Strike Zone vs RHP**

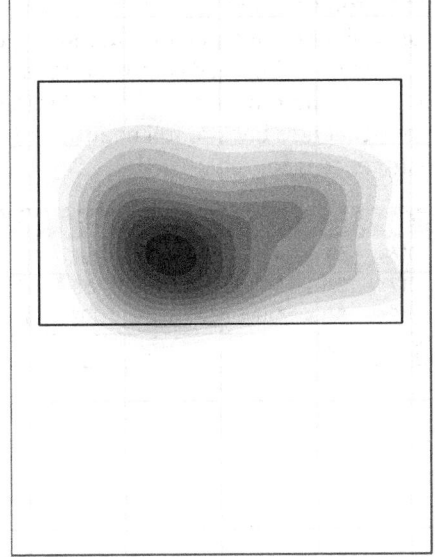

Mark Trumbo DH

Born: 01/16/86 Age: 33 Bats: R Throws: R
Height: 6'4" Weight: 225 Origin: Round 18, 2004 Draft (#533 overall)

YEAR	TEAM	LVL	AGE	PA	R	2B	3B	HR	RBI	BB	K	SB	CS	AVG/OBP/SLG
2016	BAL	MLB	30	667	94	27	1	47	108	51	170	2	0	.256/.316/.533
2017	BAL	MLB	31	603	79	22	0	23	65	42	149	1	0	.234/.289/.397
2018	BAL	MLB	32	358	41	12	0	17	44	24	87	0	0	.261/.313/.452
2019	BAL	MLB	33	506	58	21	1	20	66	40	120	1	0	.243/.307/.424

Breakout: 4% Improve: 31% Collapse: 17% Attrition: 11% MLB: 91%
Comparables: Ryan Zimmerman, Xavier Nady, Glenn Davis

Lingering knee pain shortened Trumbo's season, which had been trending in the right direction after a catastrophic 2017. Although he'll probably never scrape the lofty ceiling of his 47-home run season again, Trumbo's power numbers were well up, and not by a fluke—he was hitting the ball harder than ever, and finished the season in the top ten in all of baseball for average exit velocity. In the final year of his contract with the O's, Trumbo is slated to make $11M, and then a total of $4.5M in deferred payments after his contract ends. If Baltimore was willing to eat some of that money, they might find a willing trade partner in a contender who needs a power bat and has space at 1B/DH, thus clearing space for one of their more defensively-limited prospects. Trumbo will first need to prove that he's back to full health, and, more importantly, that his power resurgence is for real.

YEAR	TEAM	LVL	AGE	PA	DRC+	VORP	BABIP	BRR	FRAA	WARP
2016	BAL	MLB	30	667	127	18.5	.278	-2.6	RF(95): 2.2, 1B(6): 0.2	3.3
2017	BAL	MLB	31	603	87	-9.2	.278	-2.3	RF(31): -4.6, 3B(2): 0.0	-0.7
2018	BAL	MLB	32	358	102	6.4	.303	0.9	RF(19): -1.4, 1B(3): 0.2	0.6
2019	BAL	MLB	33	506	96	5.6	.283	-0.8	1B 0, RF 0	0.7

Mark Trumbo, *continued*

Batted Ball Distribution

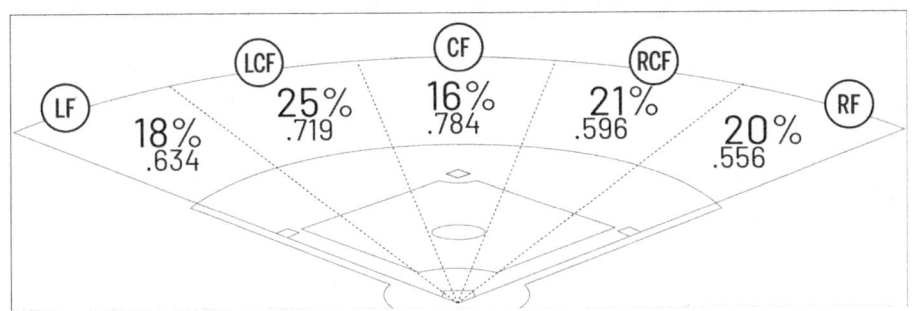

Strike Zone vs LHP

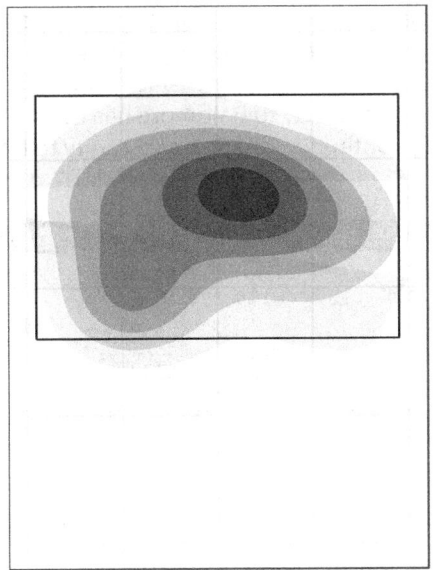

Strike Zone vs RHP

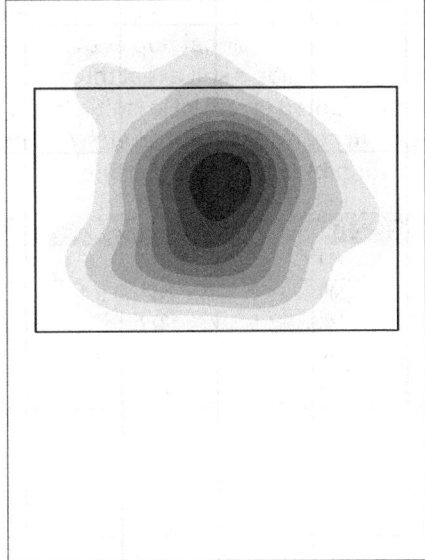

Baltimore Orioles 2019

Jonathan Villar SS
Born: 05/02/91   Age: 28   Bats: B   Throws: R
Height: 6'1"   Weight: 215   Origin: International Free Agent, 2008

YEAR	TEAM	LVL	AGE	PA	R	2B	3B	HR	RBI	BB	K	SB	CS	AVG/OBP/SLG
2016	MIL	MLB	25	679	92	38	3	19	63	79	174	62	18	.285/.369/.457
2017	MIL	MLB	26	436	49	18	1	11	40	30	132	23	8	.241/.293/.372
2018	MIL	MLB	27	279	26	10	1	6	22	19	80	14	2	.261/.315/.377
2018	BAL	MLB	27	236	28	4	0	8	24	22	58	21	3	.258/.336/.392
2019	BAL	MLB	28	565	73	22	2	14	57	47	154	36	9	.242/.308/.376

Breakout: 9%   Improve: 55%   Collapse: 12%   Attrition: 15%   MLB: 97%
Comparables: Dan Uggla, Logan Forsythe, Danny Espinosa

Villar is just two seasons removed from a year where he snuck up on the 20-homer threshold while playing middle infield, but an offensive stallout over the past two seasons cost him his job in Milwaukee, who opted to trade up by acquiring Jonathan Schoop. He may not be the toolsed-out prospect some dreamed on during his age-25 season, but he is a perfectly serviceable middle infield piece for a rebuilding club, someone who can man multiple positions and provide the occasional pop at the plate. He won't be swiping 60-plus bags, either, but Villar is still a real threat on the bases, which will be a lift for the leaden-footed Orioles. He isn't a free agent until 2021, so Baltimore has the flexibility of timing a hot stretch or a needy contender into an opportunity to flip him for prospects down the line.

YEAR	TEAM	LVL	AGE	PA	DRC+	VORP	BABIP	BRR	FRAA	WARP
2016	MIL	MLB	25	679	101	44.9	.373	-2.4	SS(108): 5.5, 3B(42): -4.1	2.7
2017	MIL	MLB	26	436	64	5.8	.330	1.6	2B(98): 2.7, CF(6): -0.1	-0.2
2018	MIL	MLB	27	279	82	6.6	.355	0.5	2B(74): -6.1	-0.3
2018	BAL	MLB	27	236	85	8.2	.319	2.4	2B(36): 1.0, SS(18): 0.5	0.8
2019	BAL	MLB	28	565	83	9.6	.313	4.4	2B -3, SS 1	1.1

Jonathan Villar, continued

Batted Ball Distribution

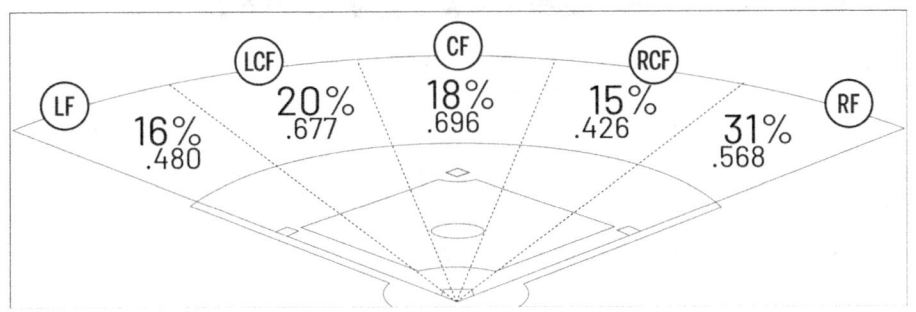

Strike Zone vs LHP   **Strike Zone vs RHP**

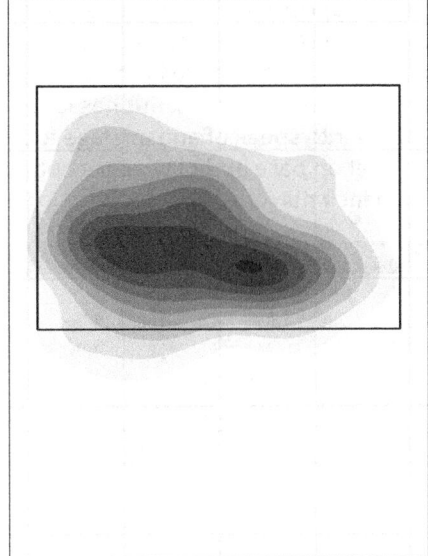

Stephen Wilkerson   INF

Born: 01/11/92   Age: 27   Bats: B   Throws: R
Height: 6'1"   Weight: 195   Origin: Round 8, 2014 Draft (#241 overall)

YEAR	TEAM	LVL	AGE	PA	R	2B	3B	HR	RBI	BB	K	SB	CS	AVG/OBP/SLG
2016	FRD	A+	24	461	49	17	4	4	36	45	98	18	6	.251/.334/.343
2017	FRD	A+	25	180	29	10	0	2	15	19	40	2	3	.323/.407/.426
2017	BOW	AA	25	273	34	13	0	6	30	20	53	5	2	.294/.354/.420
2018	NOR	AAA	26	86	13	5	0	4	13	5	15	0	1	.270/.329/.500
2018	BAL	MLB	26	49	2	3	0	0	3	3	16	1	0	.174/.224/.239
2019	BAL	MLB	27	174	19	8	1	6	21	11	40	2	1	.233/.289/.409

Breakout: 5%   Improve: 19%   Collapse: 2%   Attrition: 16%   MLB: 28%
Comparables: Hernan Iribarren, Chris Valaika, Kevin Russo

It's not unheard of for organizations to send prospects on the back nine of 25 or those with major-league experience to the Arizona Fall League, but there's usually a specific reason behind it: an injured player who needs extra reps, or a mechanical change that needs to be worked out against non-instructional-league opposition. For Wilkerson, a repeat trip to the AFL is to make up time from his 50-game PED suspension last season, as the organization attempts to suss out what they have in the utility infielder. Wilkerson has shown a solid feel for hitting in the minors, but has fallen off some in plate discipline recently. With no power to speak of and average footspeed, Wilkerson has to prove he can both get on base and play an acceptable third base in order to carve out a spot as a bench player.

YEAR	TEAM	LVL	AGE	PA	DRC+	VORP	BABIP	BRR	FRAA	WARP
2016	FRD	A+	24	461	81	4.2	.321	0.8	2B(112): -1.8, SS(1): 0.2	-0.8
2017	FRD	A+	25	180	140	11.3	.425	1.0	2B(26): -0.5, 3B(8): 0.6	1.1
2017	BOW	AA	25	273	108	11.7	.351	-0.5	3B(37): -0.6, 2B(28): 0.8	0.6
2018	NOR	AAA	26	86	117	6.0	.276	0.2	2B(10): 2.7, 3B(6): 0.3	0.6
2018	BAL	MLB	26	49	64	-3.7	.267	-0.6	2B(9): 0.9, 3B(6): 0.2	0.0
2019	BAL	MLB	27	174	79	0.8	.262	-0.2	2B 1, 3B 0	0.2

Stephen Wilkerson, continued

Batted Ball Distribution

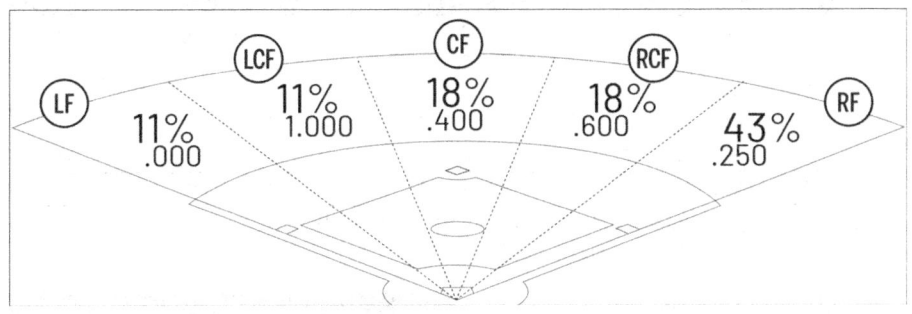

Strike Zone vs LHP   **Strike Zone vs RHP**

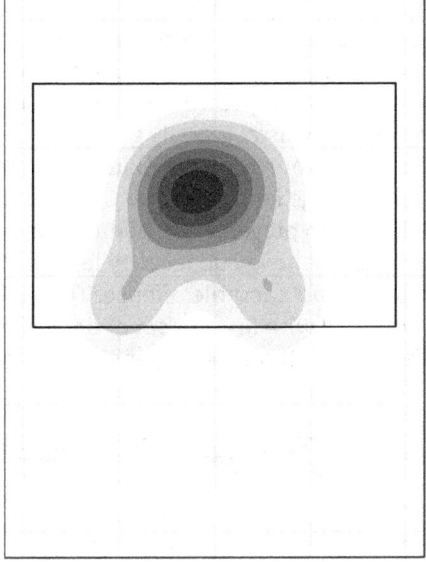

Baltimore Orioles 2019

Austin Wynns C
Born: 12/10/90 Age: 28 Bats: R Throws: R
Height: 6'2" Weight: 205 Origin: Round 10, 2013 Draft (#309 overall)

YEAR	TEAM	LVL	AGE	PA	R	2B	3B	HR	RBI	BB	K	SB	CS	AVG/OBP/SLG
2016	BOW	AA	25	82	11	7	0	0	10	7	12	1	0	.247/.309/.342
2016	FRD	A+	25	206	23	10	0	5	20	13	32	0	0	.303/.351/.436
2017	BOW	AA	26	434	54	19	1	10	46	52	64	1	0	.281/.377/.419
2018	NOR	AAA	27	153	19	4	0	4	16	11	38	0	0	.230/.288/.345
2018	BAL	MLB	27	118	16	2	0	4	11	5	25	0	0	.255/.287/.382
2019	BAL	MLB	28	231	23	7	1	7	25	15	55	0	0	.226/.281/.368

Breakout: 4% Improve: 30% Collapse: 2% Attrition: 29% MLB: 56%
Comparables: Bobby Wilson, Kyle Phillips, Dustin Garneau

In the seminal 1995 film *Showgirls*, Cristal Connors—played brilliantly by Gina Gershon, who knows exactly what kind of film she's in, even as the filmmakers apparently did not—intones from her hospital bed: "there's always someone younger and hungrier coming down the stairs after you." It's not any kind of philosophical statement; Cristal literally gets pushed down some stairs by another, younger showgirl. "Younger" is a relative term in the Orioles system, as Wynns is now 27, the same age fellow catcher Caleb Joseph was when he made his major league debut. Both players have been in the Orioles system for their entire pro careers, grinding their way up level by level with strong defensive play at a premium position and passable offense. This year, it was Wynns' turn to get his call to the Show, and with his plus set of defensive chops coupled with solid plate discipline, it looks like Wynns will be the Nomi Malone to Joseph's Cristal Connors next season.

YEAR	TEAM	P. COUNT	FRM RUNS	BLK RUNS	THRW RUNS	TOT RUNS
2017	BOW	12803	-2.2	2.7	0.5	0.6
2018	BAL	5269	-2.3	0.5	0.1	-1.8
2018	NOR	5362	0.1	-0.1	0.0	-0.3
2019	BAL	9240	-4.6	0.4	-0.3	-4.4

YEAR	TEAM	LVL	AGE	PA	DRC+	VORP	BABIP	BRR	FRAA	WARP
2016	BOW	AA	25	82	88	1.8	.290	0.1	C(20): 0.8	0.2
2016	FRD	A+	25	206	116	8.4	.340	0.4	C(36): 1.8	0.8
2017	BOW	AA	26	434	123	25.8	.314	0.6	C(92): 1.3	2.3
2018	NOR	AAA	27	153	83	3.2	.283	0.5	C(39): -1.0	0.2
2018	BAL	MLB	27	118	87	0.7	.296	-0.8	C(41): -0.5	0.3
2019	BAL	MLB	28	231	74	3.2	.267	-0.4	C -5	-0.4

Austin Wynns, continued

Batted Ball Distribution

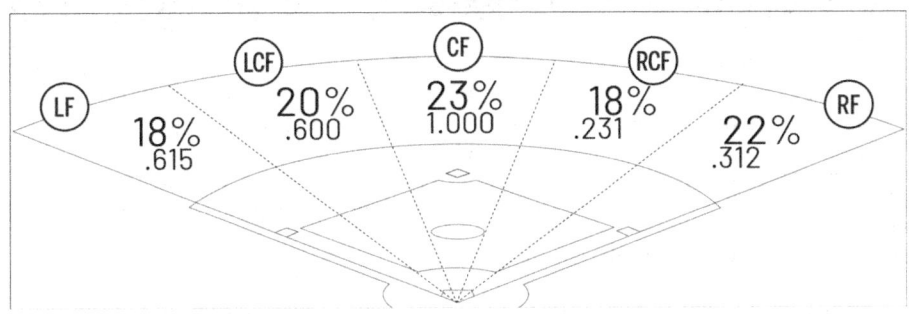

Strike Zone vs LHP **Strike Zone vs RHP**

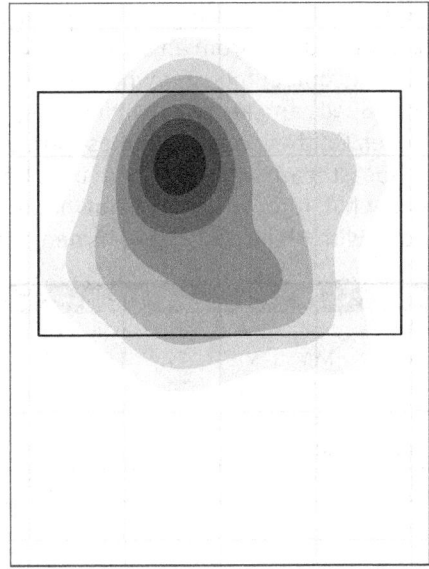

Richard Bleier LHP

Born: 04/16/87 Age: 32 Bats: L Throws: L
Height: 6'3" Weight: 215 Origin: Round 6, 2008 Draft (#183 overall)

YEAR	TEAM	LVL	AGE	W	L	SV	G	GS	IP	H	HR	BB/9	K/9	K	GB%	BABIP
2016	SWB	AAA	29	2	3	1	12	10	58	66	2	1.7	3.9	25	64%	.318
2016	NYA	MLB	29	0	0	0	23	0	23	20	0	1.6	5.1	13	55%	.270
2017	NOR	AAA	30	0	0	1	8	0	14^2	9	0	0.0	9.2	15	70%	.243
2017	BAL	MLB	30	2	1	0	57	0	63^1	62	6	1.8	3.7	26	69%	.259
2018	BAL	MLB	31	3	0	0	31	0	32^2	36	0	1.1	4.1	15	58%	.319
2019	BAL	MLB	32	2	3	0	50	0	53	56	8	3.1	5.4	32	56%	.289

Breakout: 13% Improve: 25% Collapse: 20% Attrition: 14% MLB: 55%
Comparables: Dana Eveland, Steven Wright, Dan Otero

It was a sunny day game in early June when Richard Bleier clutched his side immediately after throwing a pitch. At the time, the command-control lefty was one of the lone bright spots on an Orioles team already circling the drain. Prised from the division rival Yankees in early 2017 for cash considerations, Bleier added a cutter to his repertoire over the past two seasons. Said pitch has transformed him from an average low-velo lefty who doesn't strike anyone out to a soft-contact monster who still doesn't strike anyone out but induces a ton of groundballs and keeps the ball in the park, a valuable skill for any AL East pitcher. On that day, the Orioles were down 5-1 to the Red Sox, and the broadcast team was busy modeling the day's giveaway, an Orioles-branded bucket hat. It took them several minutes to discern something was seriously wrong with Bleier. The hat, it turned out, was reversible.

YEAR	TEAM	LVL	AGE	WHIP	ERA	DRA	WARP	MPH	FB%	WHF	CSP
2016	SWB	AAA	29	1.33	3.72	3.85	1.0				
2016	NYA	MLB	29	1.04	1.96	5.93	-0.3	91.7	61.3	9.7	43.8
2017	NOR	AAA	30	0.61	0.61	3.26	0.3				
2017	BAL	MLB	30	1.18	1.99	5.01	0.1	91.1	62.8	10	52.7
2018	BAL	MLB	31	1.22	1.93	5.09	-0.1	89.7	61.2	10	53.6
2019	BAL	MLB	32	1.40	5.32	5.03	0.1	89.8	61.5	9.9	50.4

Richard Bleier, continued

Pitch Shape vs LHH

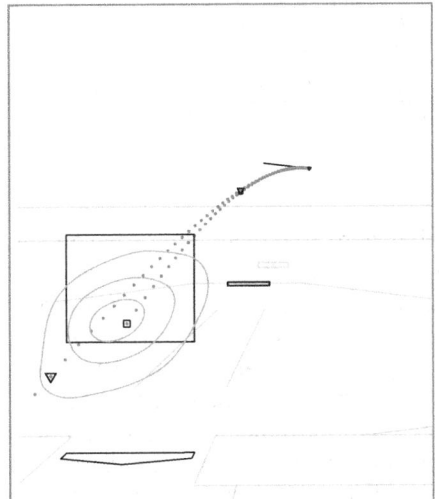

Pitch Shape vs RHH

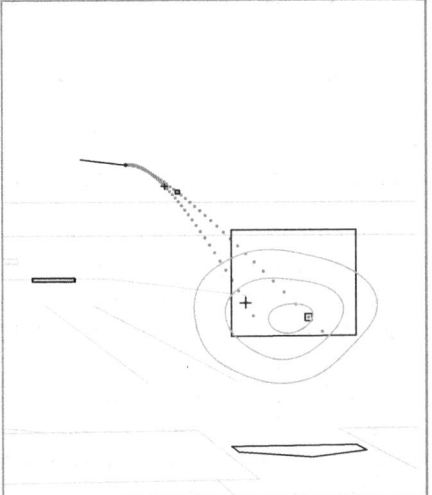

Type	Frequency	Velocity	H Movement	V Movement
● Fastball	4.4%	89.1 [89]	6.4 [101]	-24 [74]
☐ Sinker	56.8%	88.5 [80]	11.2 [111]	-28.5 [73]
+ Cutter	26.2%	86.7 [87]	0.4 [87]	-27.7 [84]
▲ Changeup	4.2%	81.8 [86]	13.5 [88]	-32.4 [85]
✕ Splitter				
▽ Slider	8.2%	79 [75]	-2.9 [91]	-40.6 [77]
◇ Curveball	0.2%	79.6 [104]	-0.1 [68]	-43.1 [111]
✦ Slow Curveball				
✱ Knuckleball				
▼ Screwball				

Dylan Bundy RHP

Born: 11/15/92 Age: 26 Bats: B Throws: R
Height: 6'1" Weight: 200 Origin: Round 1, 2011 Draft (#4 overall)

YEAR	TEAM	LVL	AGE	W	L	SV	G	GS	IP	H	HR	BB/9	K/9	K	GB%	BABIP
2016	BAL	MLB	23	10	6	0	36	14	109^2	109	18	3.4	8.5	104	37%	.299
2017	BAL	MLB	24	13	9	0	28	28	169^2	152	26	2.7	8.1	152	33%	.273
2018	BAL	MLB	25	8	16	0	31	31	171^2	188	41	2.8	9.6	184	35%	.316
2019	BAL	MLB	26	7	12	0	29	29	165^1	163	27	3.2	8.7	159	36%	.297

Breakout: 24%   Improve: 60%   Collapse: 17%   Attrition: 7%   MLB: 91%
Comparables: Oliver Perez, Floyd Bannister, Melido Perez

It's a cruelty typical of the capricious baseball gods that when Bundy wished on that monkey paw for a career-high strikeout rate, it would come along with a career-high home run rate. Pitcher wins are a poor metric, but Bundy's sharp drop in fastball velocity from 2016-2017 looks a little more worrisome when his W-L record from last season is reversed, along with the alarming spike in runs allowed. The path to the major leagues for an Orioles pitching prospect never did run smooth, but Bundy has always seemed more snakebit than most, having to battle both his own body and arcane roster construction rules to secure a place as a starter in the major leagues. He's still just 25 years old, and baseball will be a better place if the one-time Gatorade Male Athlete of the Year—the first baseball player to ever win the award—is able to deliver on his incredible promise.

YEAR	TEAM	LVL	AGE	WHIP	ERA	DRA	WARP	MPH	FB%	WHF	CSP
2016	BAL	MLB	23	1.38	4.02	5.58	-0.4	97.0	61.7	12.3	48.2
2017	BAL	MLB	24	1.20	4.24	4.93	1.2	94.0	53.8	12.3	46.4
2018	BAL	MLB	25	1.41	5.45	5.34	-0.1	93.4	55.8	13.5	50.2
2019	BAL	MLB	26	1.35	4.60	4.57	1.6	93.9	57.2	13.1	49.3

Dylan Bundy, continued

Pitch Shape vs LHH

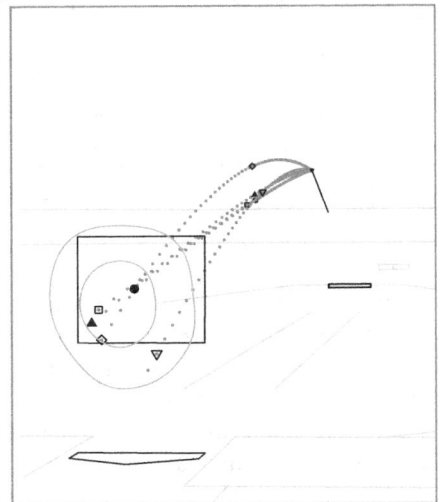

Pitch Shape vs RHH

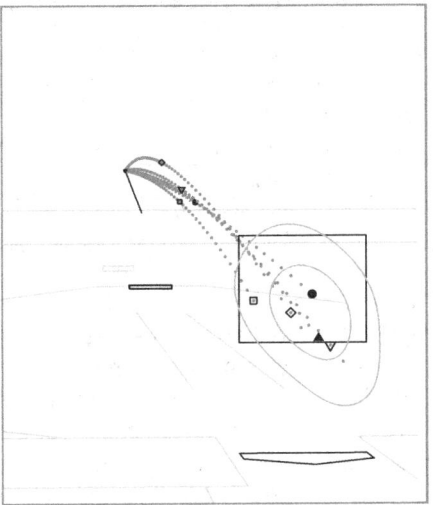

Type	Frequency	Velocity	H Movement	V Movement
● Fastball	47.7%	92 [98]	-5.7 [105]	-12.3 [111]
☐ Sinker	8.1%	91.9 [97]	-11 [113]	-15.4 [116]
+ Cutter				
▲ Changeup	10.1%	84.1 [95]	-10.4 [105]	-24.4 [109]
✕ Splitter				
▽ Slider	25.4%	81.8 [88]	4 [96]	-37.5 [87]
◇ Curveball	8.7%	75 [87]	8.1 [101]	-55.2 [84]
⊕ Slow Curveball				
✳ Knuckleball				
▼ Screwball				

Cody Carroll RHP

Born: 10/15/92 Age: 26 Bats: R Throws: R
Height: 6'5" Weight: 215 Origin: Round 22, 2015 Draft (#663 overall)

YEAR	TEAM	LVL	AGE	W	L	SV	G	GS	IP	H	HR	BB/9	K/9	K	GB%	BABIP
2016	CSC	A	23	4	4	3	26	6	91^1	89	3	4.0	8.9	90	51%	.336
2017	TAM	A+	24	1	0	2	13	0	20	10	1	3.6	13.5	30	39%	.225
2017	TRN	AA	24	2	5	5	26	0	47^1	36	4	4.2	11.2	59	48%	.291
2018	SWB	AAA	25	3	0	9	32	0	41^2	27	0	3.9	11.9	55	34%	.287
2018	BAL	MLB	25	0	2	0	15	0	17	21	6	6.9	8.5	16	33%	.306
2019	BAL	MLB	26	2	3	0	45	0	47	46	7	5.2	9.3	49	41%	.298

Breakout: 15% Improve: 23% Collapse: 10% Attrition: 22% MLB: 39%
Comparables: Angel Nesbitt, Juan Minaya, Jose Valdez

The Orioles got three MLB-adjacent pitchers in return for Zach Britton, including big (6'5") righty Carroll. The 2015 22nd-rounder made steady progress through the Yankees system, although his walk rate has always been a slight concern. Carroll has a big fastball that regularly sits in the upper-90s and can graze triple digits, and he pairs that with a hard, tightly-spinning slider that profiles as a plus pitch. Carroll also throws a splitter that's less developed than his other two pitches. The Orioles are shaping up to have a bullpen full of hard-throwing, poor-command pitchers; AL East hitters might be well-served to invest in all manner of protective gear this off-season.

YEAR	TEAM	LVL	AGE	WHIP	ERA	DRA	WARP	MPH	FB%	WHF	CSP
2016	CSC	A	23	1.42	3.15	3.35	1.6				
2017	TAM	A+	24	0.90	2.25	3.00	0.4				
2017	TRN	AA	24	1.23	2.66	2.50	1.3				
2018	SWB	AAA	25	1.08	2.38	2.64	1.2				
2018	BAL	MLB	25	2.00	9.00	8.32	-0.7	97.6	66.4	8.9	44.9
2019	BAL	MLB	26	1.54	5.43	5.11	0.0	97.2	67.6	9	45.7

Cody Carroll, continued

Pitch Shape vs LHH

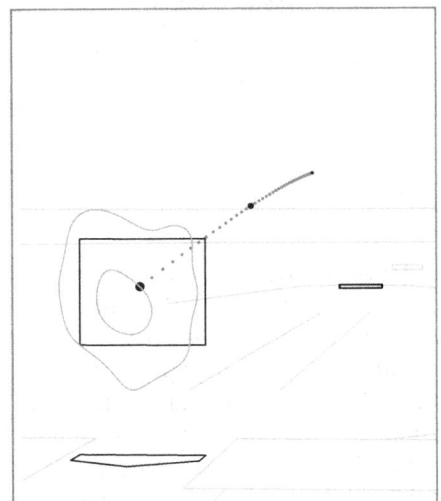

Pitch Shape vs RHH

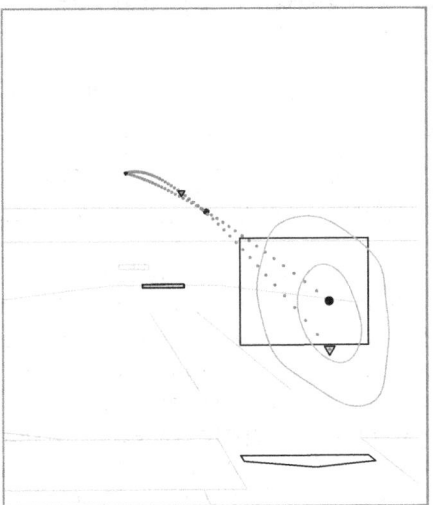

Type	Frequency	Velocity	H Movement	V Movement
● Fastball	66.4%	96.5 [113]	-4.5 [110]	-10.8 [116]
☐ Sinker				
+ Cutter				
▲ Changeup				
✕ Splitter	5.9%	87.1 [108]	-4.4 [114]	-28 [106]
▽ Slider	27.7%	83.7 [97]	5.6 [103]	-38.4 [84]
◇ Curveball				
✦ Slow Curveball				
✳ Knuckleball				
▼ Screwball				

Andrew Cashner RHP

Born: 09/11/86 Age: 32 Bats: R Throws: R
Height: 6'6" Weight: 235 Origin: Round 1, 2008 Draft (#19 overall)

YEAR	TEAM	LVL	AGE	W	L	SV	G	GS	IP	H	HR	BB/9	K/9	K	GB%	BABIP
2016	SDN	MLB	29	4	7	0	16	16	79^1	80	13	3.4	7.6	67	49%	.291
2016	MIA	MLB	29	1	4	0	12	11	52^2	62	6	5.1	7.7	45	47%	.352
2017	TEX	MLB	30	11	11	0	28	28	166^2	156	15	3.5	4.6	86	49%	.266
2018	BAL	MLB	31	4	15	0	28	28	153	177	25	3.8	5.8	99	42%	.311
2019	BAL	MLB	32	5	12	0	26	26	137	157	24	4.0	5.7	88	44%	.297

Breakout: 6% Improve: 38% Collapse: 26% Attrition: 9% MLB: 86%
Comparables: Jon Garland, Yovani Gallardo, Jeff Suppan

Cashner parlayed a strong 2017 for the Rangers into a two-year, $16MM contract with Baltimore. At the time, the O's rotation consisted of Bundy, Gausman, and three tallboys of Natty Boh, so it was easy enough to paper over Cashner's poor peripherals and focus instead on his shiny 3.40 ERA. Unsurprisingly, that strategy has backfired, and Cashner's numbers look awful no matter which lens one chooses to apply. A special low point came in early August, when Cashner set an Orioles record by surrendering 10 runs in fewer than two innings, an impressive achievement in considering both the history of the Orioles and the history of Orioles pitching. Maybe Baltimore's FO knew exactly what they were doing in signing Cashner to be an innings sponge for two years of a rebuilding team, just like maybe Alexander Fleming knew exactly what he was doing when he left those dishes in the sink and discovered penicillin. Crazy like a fox, those Orioles.

YEAR	TEAM	LVL	AGE	WHIP	ERA	DRA	WARP	MPH	FB%	WHF	CSP
2016	SDN	MLB	29	1.39	4.76	6.24	-0.8	97.2	66.6	7.8	46.6
2016	MIA	MLB	29	1.75	5.98	6.04	-0.4	96.6	66.6	8.1	44.3
2017	TEX	MLB	30	1.32	3.40	5.58	0.0	96.0	65.1	6.7	49.6
2018	BAL	MLB	31	1.58	5.29	6.69	-2.4	94.8	60.2	7.5	46.7
2019	BAL	MLB	32	1.59	5.67	5.69	-0.4	94.7	62.8	7.2	47

Andrew Cashner, continued

Pitch Shape vs LHH	Pitch Shape vs RHH
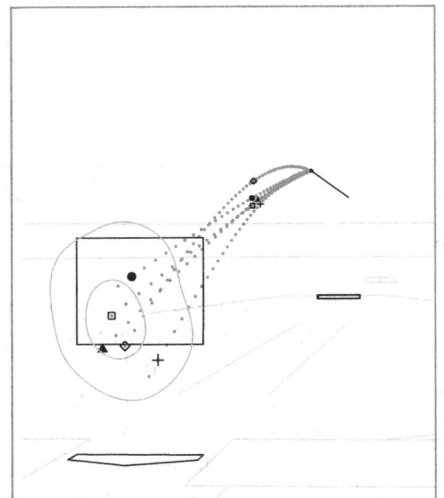	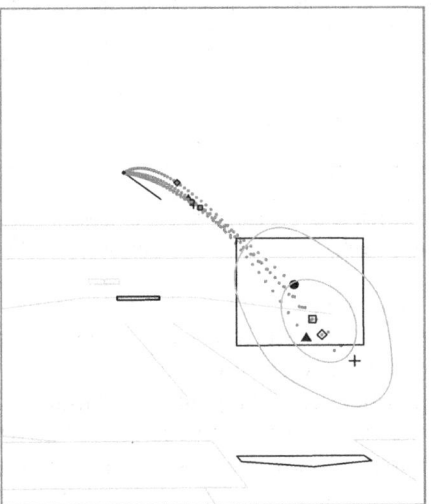

Type	Frequency	Velocity	H Movement	V Movement
● Fastball	24.4%	93.6 [103]	-7.3 [97]	-13 [109]
□ Sinker	35.8%	92.3 [99]	-12.1 [104]	-16.8 [112]
+ Cutter	13.8%	86 [84]	2.3 [102]	-28.7 [80]
▲ Changeup	13.3%	84.1 [95]	-11.1 [101]	-27.8 [99]
× Splitter				
▽ Slider				
◇ Curveball	12.7%	81.2 [110]	5.9 [92]	-44.1 [109]
✦ Slow Curveball				
✳ Knuckleball				
▼ Screwball				

Miguel Castro   RHP

Born: 12/24/94   Age: 24   Bats: R   Throws: R
Height: 6'7"   Weight: 205   Origin: International Free Agent, 2012

YEAR	TEAM	LVL	AGE	W	L	SV	G	GS	IP	H	HR	BB/9	K/9	K	GB%	BABIP
2016	COL	MLB	21	0	0	0	19	0	14²	18	3	3.1	7.4	12	55%	.326
2016	ABQ	AAA	21	2	3	0	16	0	15²	21	5	4.0	8.6	15	49%	.364
2017	BOW	AA	22	3	0	0	6	0	24¹	23	1	2.2	4.1	11	49%	.275
2017	BAL	MLB	22	3	3	0	39	1	66¹	53	8	3.8	5.2	38	50%	.227
2018	BAL	MLB	23	2	7	0	63	1	86¹	75	9	5.2	5.9	57	49%	.259
2019	BAL	MLB	24	3	4	0	67	0	70	68	9	4.9	6.8	53	47%	.279

Breakout: 23%   Improve: 44%   Collapse: 23%   Attrition: 18%   MLB: 88%
Comparables: Anibal Sanchez, Trevor Gott, Oscar Villarreal

Cheap, fast, or quality: the old adage in sales is that you can have two, but never all three. Castro is cheap, having been acquired off waivers in 2017 from the Rockies, and he throws his fastball very fast, but this year he posted dismal peripherals, walking almost as many batters as he struck out. Castro has been in organized baseball since 2012, when a triple-digit fastball was more of a unicorn than it is today; he's no longer the youngest nor the hardest thrower, and if he can't solve his command issues, it's hard to project him in the back end of anyone's bullpen, even the lowly Orioles. Castro will hit arbitration in 2020, so the clock is ticking on the "cheap" part of the trifecta, which is, unfortunately, the only compelling part of his value until he learns to throw more quality strikes.

YEAR	TEAM	LVL	AGE	WHIP	ERA	DRA	WARP	MPH	FB%	WHF	CSP
2016	COL	MLB	21	1.57	6.14	4.96	0.0	98.9	57.3	11.7	46.5
2016	ABQ	AAA	21	1.79	10.34	5.28	-0.1				
2017	BOW	AA	22	1.19	4.44	3.80	0.3				
2017	BAL	MLB	22	1.22	3.53	5.51	-0.2	98.3	61.4	10.5	45.9
2018	BAL	MLB	23	1.45	3.96	6.49	-1.5	98.2	58.1	10.4	47.8
2019	BAL	MLB	24	1.49	5.61	5.24	-0.1	98.1	61	10.8	48.3

Miguel Castro, continued

Pitch Shape vs LHH

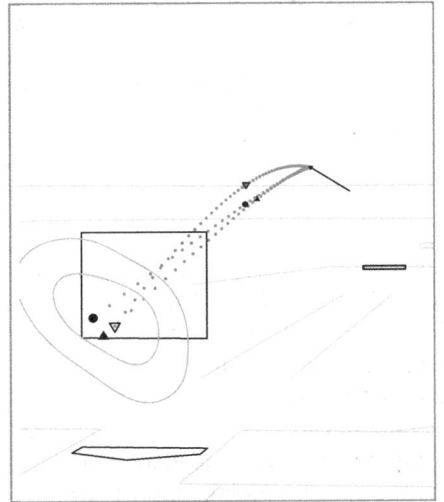

Pitch Shape vs RHH

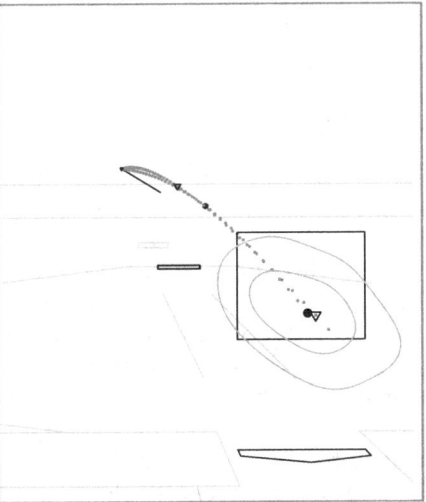

Type	Frequency	Velocity	H Movement	V Movement
● Fastball	58.1%	95.9 [111]	-14.6 [64]	-18.9 [90]
☐ Sinker				
+ Cutter				
▲ Changeup	15.7%	88.3 [112]	-15 [80]	-25.3 [106]
✕ Splitter				
▽ Slider	26.2%	84.7 [101]	6.2 [106]	-33.9 [97]
◇ Curveball				
⊕ Slow Curveball				
✻ Knuckleball				
▼ Screwball				

Alex Cobb RHP

Born: 10/07/87   Age: 31   Bats: R   Throws: R
Height: 6'3"   Weight: 205   Origin: Round 4, 2006 Draft (#109 overall)

YEAR	TEAM	LVL	AGE	W	L	SV	G	GS	IP	H	HR	BB/9	K/9	K	GB%	BABIP
2016	DUR	AAA	28	0	1	0	4	4	15	24	3	3.0	6.0	10	44%	.389
2016	TBA	MLB	28	1	2	0	5	5	22	32	5	2.9	6.5	16	52%	.355
2017	TBA	MLB	29	12	10	0	29	29	179^1	175	22	2.2	6.4	128	49%	.282
2018	BAL	MLB	30	5	15	0	28	28	152^1	172	24	2.5	6.0	102	51%	.303
2019	BAL	MLB	31	6	13	0	29	29	153^2	172	24	3.1	5.7	97	48%	.296

Breakout: 9%   Improve: 57%   Collapse: 22%   Attrition: 8%   MLB: 96%
Comparables: Ivan Nova, Kyle Lohse, Homer Bailey

Tommy John surgery robbed Cobb of his elite split-change, which didn't have the same movement when he brought back the pitch in 2017. After a slow start to the season, Cobb steadily improved month to month as the pitch once nicknamed "The Thing" started showing signs of life; from June to August, he nearly tripled the number of whiffs induced on the splitter. Cobb's improvement wasn't as stark as his first half (6.41) vs. second half (2.56) ERA would have you believe, but the peripherals improved enough to call it a bounceback from his early-season struggles. It's almost like having a spring training matters. While other teams guarded their purse strings jealously last off-season, the Orioles handed Cobb the third-largest contract for a pitcher in free agency that year, so a return to form is important for both Cobb and for his future trade value if the Orioles continue to flounder.

YEAR	TEAM	LVL	AGE	WHIP	ERA	DRA	WARP	MPH	FB%	WHF	CSP
2016	DUR	AAA	28	1.93	6.60	6.57	-0.2				
2016	TBA	MLB	28	1.77	8.59	4.56	0.2	92.5	48.2	8	47.1
2017	TBA	MLB	29	1.22	3.66	4.07	3.0	93.0	51.5	7.5	47
2018	BAL	MLB	30	1.41	4.90	5.50	-0.3	93.2	51.5	8	47.6
2019	BAL	MLB	31	1.47	5.18	5.17	0.5	92.2	51	7.7	47

Alex Cobb, continued

Pitch Shape vs LHH

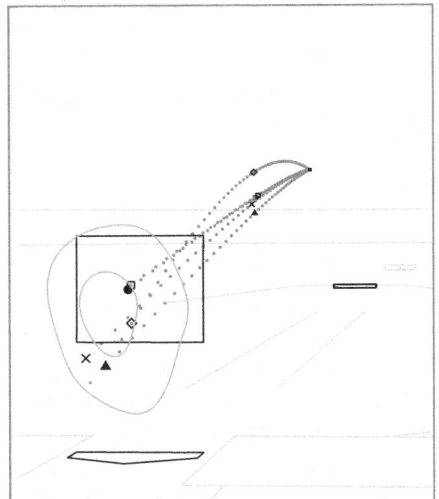

Pitch Shape vs RHH

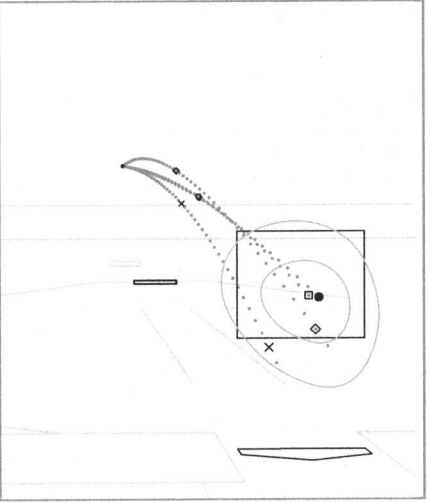

Type	Frequency	Velocity	H Movement	V Movement
● Fastball	9.3%	92.6 [100]	-9.4 [88]	-14.5 [104]
□ Sinker	42.1%	92.3 [99]	-11.8 [107]	-15.9 [114]
+ Cutter				
▲ Changeup	3.6%	87 [107]	-13.4 [89]	-24 [110]
✕ Splitter	22.9%	86.8 [106]	-12.3 [84]	-25.8 [116]
▽ Slider				
◇ Curveball	22.0%	81.9 [113]	3.9 [83]	-50.3 [95]
✦ Slow Curveball				
✱ Knuckleball				
▼ Screwball				

Baltimore Orioles 2019

Mychal Givens   RHP
Born: 05/13/90   Age: 29   Bats: R   Throws: R
Height: 6'0"   Weight: 210   Origin: Round 2, 2009 Draft (#54 overall)

YEAR	TEAM	LVL	AGE	W	L	SV	G	GS	IP	H	HR	BB/9	K/9	K	GB%	BABIP
2016	BAL	MLB	26	8	2	0	66	0	74²	59	6	4.3	11.6	96	38%	.314
2017	BAL	MLB	27	8	1	0	69	0	78²	57	10	2.9	10.1	88	43%	.251
2018	BAL	MLB	28	0	7	9	69	0	76²	61	4	3.5	9.3	79	38%	.284
2019	BAL	MLB	29	3	3	25	61	0	64²	59	10	4.0	9.3	67	40%	.290

Breakout: 19%   Improve: 40%   Collapse: 31%   Attrition: 17%   MLB: 89%
Comparables: Hunter Strickland, Justin Wilson, A.J. Ramos

Baltimore is one of America's best, most underrated cities, so if Givens wanted to remain there this season—and who wouldn't, when the alternatives were Houston or Cleveland or Arizona—he went about it exactly the right way. By posting an almost perfectly average performance for an AL reliever, Givens did enough to ensure his job security, but not so much as to tempt other teams who came sniffing around at the trade deadline. Closer by default after the Orioles started selling off bullpen pieces, Givens is arbitration-eligible in 2019 in a system that rewards saves, and wound up as Baltimore's most valuable pitcher, which will inflate his price tag. Now that the Orioles have flipped the hyperdrive switch on a rebuild, it wouldn't be surprising to see the 28-year-old moved this off-season to a team that values his ability to keep the ball in the park and won't mind paying closer prices for him in arbitration. Hopefully, he likes the neighborhood.

YEAR	TEAM	LVL	AGE	WHIP	ERA	DRA	WARP	MPH	FB%	WHF	CSP
2016	BAL	MLB	26	1.27	3.13	3.51	1.3	97.3	63.5	16	49.9
2017	BAL	MLB	27	1.04	2.75	3.69	1.3	97.8	72.2	13.1	50.3
2018	BAL	MLB	28	1.19	3.99	4.84	0.1	97.3	76.8	12.5	53.1
2019	BAL	MLB	29	1.36	4.54	4.45	0.5	96.8	71.8	13.6	51.4

Mychal Givens, continued

Pitch Shape vs LHH

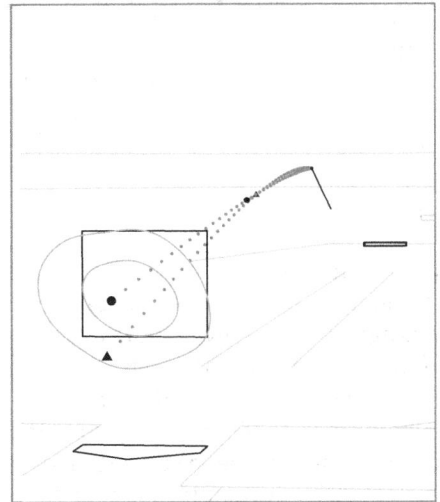

Pitch Shape vs RHH

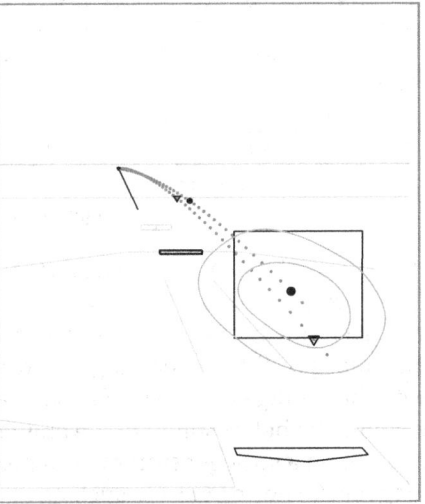

Type	Frequency	Velocity	H Movement	V Movement
● Fastball	76.7%	95.6 [110]	-6.8 [99]	-16.1 [99]
☐ Sinker				
+ Cutter				
▲ Changeup	9.0%	86.6 [105]	-9.8 [108]	-36.2 [74]
✕ Splitter				
▽ Slider	14.2%	86.8 [111]	5.6 [103]	-29.8 [109]
◇ Curveball				
⬥ Slow Curveball				
✷ Knuckleball				
▼ Screwball				

Orioles Player Analysis - 55

David Hess RHP

Born: 07/10/93   Age: 25   Bats: R   Throws: R
Height: 6'2"   Weight: 180   Origin: Round 5, 2014 Draft (#151 overall)

YEAR	TEAM	LVL	AGE	W	L	SV	G	GS	IP	H	HR	BB/9	K/9	K	GB%	BABIP
2016	BOW	AA	22	5	13	0	25	24	127^1	162	19	2.8	6.0	85	36%	.335
2017	BOW	AA	23	11	9	0	27	26	154^1	137	16	3.1	7.2	123	32%	.269
2018	NOR	AAA	24	3	2	0	9	9	45^2	38	3	3.7	8.7	44	29%	.285
2018	BAL	MLB	24	3	10	0	21	19	103^1	106	22	3.2	6.4	74	35%	.268
2019	BAL	MLB	25	4	9	0	19	19	100^2	112	21	3.4	6.7	75	34%	.291

Breakout: 8%   Improve: 18%   Collapse: 13%   Attrition: 16%   MLB: 36%
Comparables: Shairon Martis, Barry Enright, Justin Grimm

Hess was on his way to a solid start at Triple-A before being unceremoniously flung into the O's starting rotation. Unsurprisingly, the 25-year-old righty, who struggled to adjust to Double-A two seasons ago, struggled even more against major league hitters. The fringey nature of Hess's secondary offerings combined with the average velo on his fastball have led some scouts to ponder if he wouldn't be better suited to the bullpen, where his fastball might play up to the mid-90s. In a stronger system, he'd probably have already been converted to long relief. The key to Hess sticking as a starter will be developing his changeup into a major league-quality pitch, but he's still a flyball pitcher in the AL East, baseball's equivalent of the passenger pigeon.

YEAR	TEAM	LVL	AGE	WHIP	ERA	DRA	WARP	MPH	FB%	WHF	CSP
2016	BOW	AA	22	1.58	5.37	5.80	-1.1				
2017	BOW	AA	23	1.23	3.85	5.73	-1.1				
2018	NOR	AAA	24	1.25	3.15	3.96	0.8				
2018	BAL	MLB	24	1.38	4.88	7.38	-2.5	94.1	58.7	9.1	47.9
2019	BAL	MLB	25	1.48	5.76	5.79	-0.4	93.8	60.1	9.3	49

David Hess, continued

Pitch Shape vs LHH

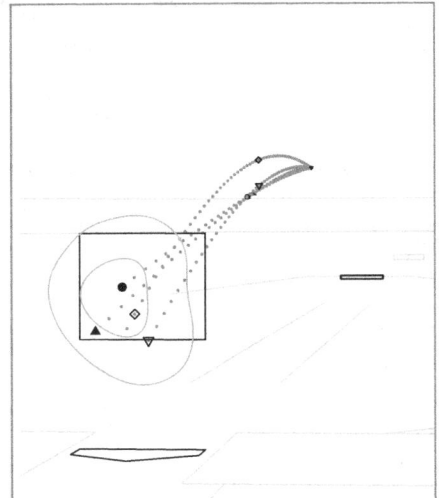

Pitch Shape vs RHH

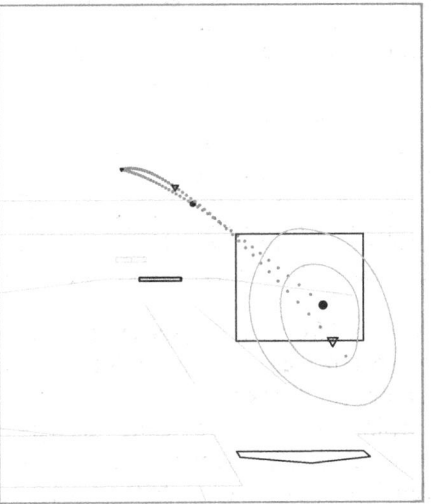

Type	Frequency	Velocity	H Movement	V Movement
● Fastball	58.6%	92.3 [99]	-2.3 [120]	-13.7 [107]
□ Sinker	0.2%	93.5 [105]	-12.7 [99]	-14.6 [119]
+ Cutter				
▲ Changeup	9.0%	84 [95]	-8.7 [113]	-26.9 [101]
× Splitter				
▽ Slider	24.9%	80.3 [81]	6.8 [108]	-36.1 [91]
◇ Curveball	7.4%	72.5 [78]	10.8 [112]	-54.8 [85]
⊕ Slow Curveball				
✳ Knuckleball				
▼ Screwball				

Yefrey Ramirez   RHP

Born: 11/28/93   Age: 25   Bats: R   Throws: R
Height: 6'2"   Weight: 215   Origin: International Free Agent, 2011

YEAR	TEAM	LVL	AGE	W	L	SV	G	GS	IP	H	HR	BB/9	K/9	K	GB%	BABIP
2016	CSC	A	22	4	2	0	11	11	61	48	4	2.1	9.7	66	40%	.272
2016	TAM	A+	22	3	7	0	11	11	63^1	34	5	2.6	9.4	66	42%	.195
2017	TRN	AA	23	10	3	0	18	18	92^1	78	9	3.7	8.9	91	36%	.284
2017	BOW	AA	23	5	0	0	6	6	32	27	6	3.1	7.3	26	28%	.250
2018	NOR	AAA	24	3	5	0	14	14	72	62	7	2.8	9.0	72	35%	.282
2018	BAL	MLB	24	1	8	0	17	12	65^1	64	11	5.0	8.5	62	36%	.293
2019	BAL	MLB	25	2	3	0	22	5	42^2	41	7	3.7	8.4	40	36%	.286

Breakout: 15%   Improve: 44%   Collapse: 25%   Attrition: 41%   MLB: 80%
Comparables: Tyler Thornburg, Robert Stephenson, Aaron Blair

Acquired from the Yankees but D-Backs raised
In Norfolk was where he spent most of his days
Chilling out max and relaxing all fine
Upping Ks and dropping his walks per nine
When a couple of starters, their arms got fatigued
And Yefry got called up to the big leagues
He had a few little scuffles against the Yankees
The Orioles didn't have options, to put it quite frankly
But the changeup is plus and the fastball's alive
And in the O's rotation, that's good enough for #5.

YEAR	TEAM	LVL	AGE	WHIP	ERA	DRA	WARP	MPH	FB%	WHF	CSP
2016	CSC	A	22	1.02	2.80	2.67	1.7				
2016	TAM	A+	22	0.82	2.84	2.46	2.2				
2017	TRN	AA	23	1.26	3.41	3.57	1.8				
2017	BOW	AA	23	1.19	3.66	4.06	0.4				
2018	NOR	AAA	24	1.17	3.88	4.39	0.9				
2018	BAL	MLB	24	1.53	5.92	6.93	-1.3	94.8	51.8	11.9	44.2
2019	BAL	MLB	25	1.36	5.15	5.01	0.1	94.5	53.1	12.1	45.2

Yefrey Ramirez, continued

Pitch Shape vs LHH

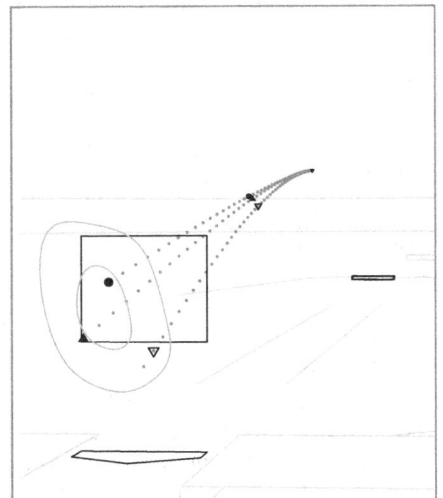

Pitch Shape vs RHH

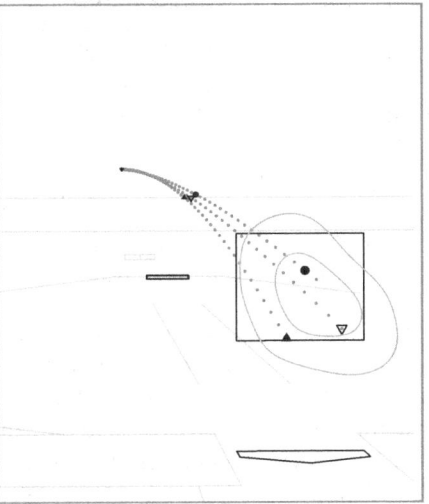

Type	Frequency	Velocity	H Movement	V Movement
● Fastball	48.4%	92.9 [101]	-8.1 [94]	-13.8 [106]
☐ Sinker	3.4%	92 [98]	-13 [96]	-18.8 [105]
+ Cutter				
▲ Changeup	25.5%	86.3 [104]	-13.1 [90]	-26.9 [101]
✕ Splitter				
▽ Slider	22.6%	87.5 [114]	1.9 [87]	-25.6 [122]
◇ Curveball				
⊕ Slow Curveball				
✳ Knuckleball				
▼ Screwball				

Baltimore Orioles 2019

Tanner Scott LHP

Born: 07/22/94 Age: 24 Bats: R Throws: L
Height: 6'2" Weight: 220 Origin: Round 6, 2014 Draft (#181 overall)

YEAR	TEAM	LVL	AGE	W	L	SV	G	GS	IP	H	HR	BB/9	K/9	K	GB%	BABIP
2016	FRD	A+	21	4	2	5	29	0	48^1	22	1	7.8	11.7	63	59%	.198
2016	BOW	AA	21	1	2	0	14	0	16	18	0	8.4	10.1	18	64%	.429
2017	BOW	AA	22	0	2	0	24	24	69	45	2	6.0	11.3	87	54%	.281
2017	BAL	MLB	22	0	0	0	2	0	1^2	2	0	10.8	10.8	2	20%	.400
2018	NOR	AAA	23	0	1	0	10	0	12	10	0	6.8	9.8	13	62%	.345
2018	BAL	MLB	23	3	3	0	53	0	53^1	55	6	4.7	12.8	76	49%	.380
2019	BAL	MLB	24	2	3	0	50	0	53	44	5	6.7	11.1	65	50%	.299

Breakout: 24%   Improve: 32%   Collapse: 13%   Attrition: 20%   MLB: 55%
Comparables: Cam Bedrosian, Carlos Estevez, Manny Delcarmen

Triple-digit hurlers with poor command are baseball's Furbys, but Scott adds a wrinkle in throwing from the left side. He's never had a BB% below double-digits, though his ability to miss bats has helped mitigate the high walk rate in the minors. In the majors, Scott surrendered six home runs in just over 50 innings, twice the number he gave up over his entire minor league career, and his willingness to hand out free passes means those big flies turned into Earl Weaver Specials. With his plus fastball and wipeout slider, Scott can get away with either an elevated walk rate or the occasional solo shot, but not both. There are worse arms to dream on, but the O's might be smart to deal Scott this off-season and let some other team work out the command problems that have plagued him throughout his pro career.

YEAR	TEAM	LVL	AGE	WHIP	ERA	DRA	WARP	MPH	FB%	WHF	CSP
2016	FRD	A+	21	1.32	4.47	5.88	-0.4				
2016	BOW	AA	21	2.06	5.62	3.64	0.2				
2017	BOW	AA	22	1.32	2.22	4.12	0.9				
2017	BAL	MLB	22	2.40	10.80	2.36	0.1	100.1	70.3	10.8	29.6
2018	NOR	AAA	23	1.58	0.75	3.47	0.2				
2018	BAL	MLB	23	1.56	5.40	2.85	1.3	98.6	55.3	18	43.3
2019	BAL	MLB	24	1.56	4.44	4.39	0.5	98.4	57.4	18.3	38.3

Tanner Scott, continued

Pitch Shape vs LHH

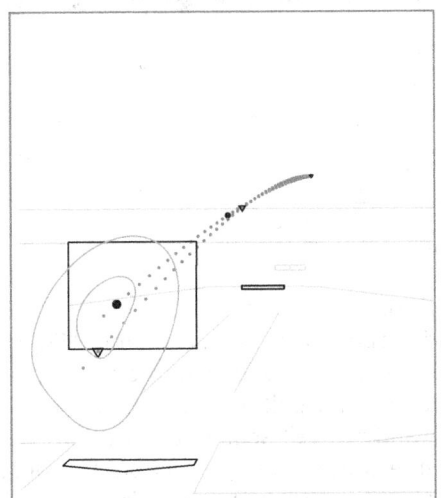

Pitch Shape vs RHH

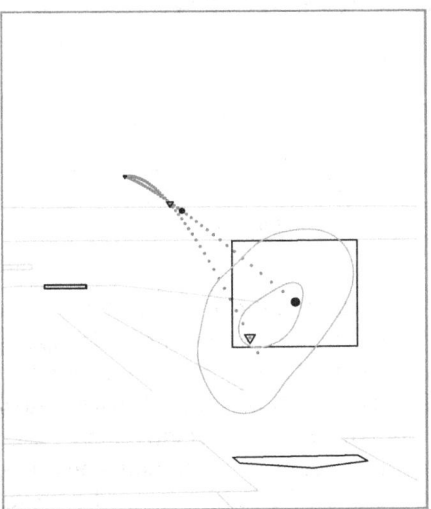

Type	Frequency	Velocity	H Movement	V Movement
● Fastball	55.3%	97.4 [116]	6.7 [100]	-13.2 [108]
☐ Sinker				
+ Cutter				
▲ Changeup				
✕ Splitter				
▽ Slider	44.7%	89 [120]	-3.4 [93]	-30.8 [106]
◇ Curveball				
✦ Slow Curveball				
✱ Knuckleball				
▼ Screwball				

Mike Wright   RHP

Born: 01/03/90   Age: 29   Bats: R   Throws: R
Height: 6'6"   Weight: 215   Origin: Round 3, 2011 Draft (#94 overall)

YEAR	TEAM	LVL	AGE	W	L	SV	G	GS	IP	H	HR	BB/9	K/9	K	GB%	BABIP
2016	NOR	AAA	26	4	4	0	13	13	76[1]	72	8	1.7	5.7	48	45%	.272
2016	BAL	MLB	26	3	4	0	18	12	74[2]	81	12	3.1	6.0	50	43%	.299
2017	NOR	AAA	27	4	6	0	16	16	83	81	6	2.8	7.7	71	46%	.301
2017	BAL	MLB	27	0	0	0	13	0	25	26	5	2.5	10.1	28	44%	.318
2018	BAL	MLB	28	4	2	0	48	2	84[1]	101	12	3.8	7.9	74	37%	.344
2019	BAL	MLB	29	2	3	0	50	0	53	54	8	3.5	7.6	45	41%	.292

Breakout: 20%   Improve: 32%   Collapse: 19%   Attrition: 24%   MLB: 56%
Comparables: Josh Hancock, Jeremy Hefner, Tom Koehler

At the dawn of the Industrial Revolution, the circumstances of one's birth determined one's fate. Hit the jackpot and get born into a wealthy family? Enjoy your Grand Tour, bedsheets warmed by your personal valet, and rerouting train lines so the smoke doesn't belch onto your personal golf course. Born into a poor family? Best develop a taste for gruel and get well-acquainted with the inner workings of a spinning jenny. The same, unfortunately, describes the lot of those drafted by clubs trapped in a cycle of futility. Wright has been in the Orioles system since 2011, bouncing between Triple-A and the big club for the past four seasons, and looks bound for the same sort of existence next season. Sometimes you're the spinning jenny, sometimes you're the pitching prospect that gets ground under its wheels for the better part of a decade.

YEAR	TEAM	LVL	AGE	WHIP	ERA	DRA	WARP	MPH	FB%	WHF	CSP
2016	NOR	AAA	26	1.13	3.07	3.86	1.3				
2016	BAL	MLB	26	1.43	5.79	7.13	-1.6	96.5	70.1	7.4	47.9
2017	NOR	AAA	27	1.29	3.69	4.20	1.4				
2017	BAL	MLB	27	1.32	5.76	4.41	0.2	96.2	61.2	11.3	45.3
2018	BAL	MLB	28	1.62	5.55	6.60	-1.6	96.5	58.2	9.1	48.7
2019	BAL	MLB	29	1.40	5.15	4.90	0.2	95.8	62	8.9	47.4

Mike Wright, continued

Pitch Shape vs LHH

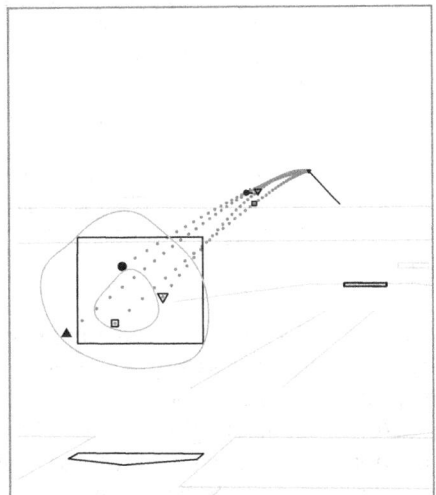

Pitch Shape vs RHH

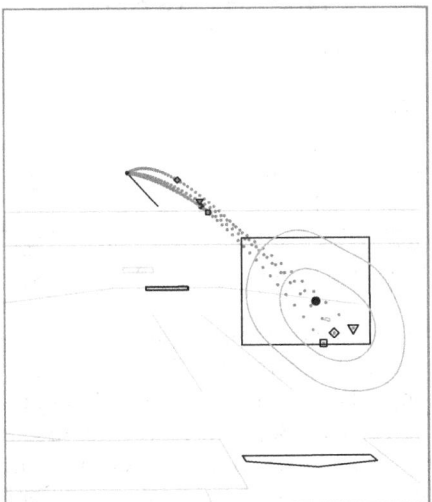

Type	Frequency	Velocity	H Movement	V Movement
● Fastball	39.9%	94.1 [105]	-6.7 [100]	-14.4 [104]
□ Sinker	18.3%	92.6 [101]	-14 [88]	-21.6 [96]
+ Cutter				
▲ Changeup	5.3%	83.1 [91]	-13.3 [89]	-29.4 [94]
✕ Splitter				
▽ Slider	30.1%	89.9 [124]	2.6 [90]	-25.5 [122]
◇ Curveball	6.4%	78.6 [101]	6.5 [94]	-43.2 [111]
⊕ Slow Curveball				
✳ Knuckleball				
▼ Screwball				

Jimmy Yacabonis RHP

Born: 03/21/92   Age: 27   Bats: R   Throws: R
Height: 6'3"   Weight: 205   Origin: Round 13, 2013 Draft (#399 overall)

YEAR	TEAM	LVL	AGE	W	L	SV	G	GS	IP	H	HR	BB/9	K/9	K	GB%	BABIP
2016	FRD	A+	24	0	2	5	16	0	20^1	17	2	2.7	9.3	21	43%	.278
2016	BOW	AA	24	2	2	6	34	0	44^1	34	2	2.8	9.3	46	57%	.271
2017	NOR	AAA	25	4	0	11	41	0	61^1	30	0	4.1	7.0	48	49%	.184
2017	BAL	MLB	25	2	0	0	14	0	20^2	18	2	6.1	3.5	8	47%	.242
2018	NOR	AAA	26	3	5	0	21	21	76	61	6	3.8	7.3	62	46%	.258
2018	BAL	MLB	26	0	2	0	12	7	40	40	8	4.1	7.4	33	43%	.283
2019	BAL	MLB	27	2	3	0	22	5	42^2	43	6	4.2	7.0	33	46%	.290

Breakout: 10%   Improve: 18%   Collapse: 13%   Attrition: 15%   MLB: 34%
Comparables: Kanekoa Texeira, Logan Ondrusek, Pedro Beato

After relieving for his entire professional career, the O's transitioned Jimmy Yaks to starter this year in Triple-A before calling him up to serve as a spot starter/long reliever. The combined 116 innings he pitched this season were a career-high by over 30, so in evaluating Yacaboneyard's season, it might be more fair to give it an "in progress" rather than a harsh letter grade. The fastball still has a lot of late life and the carnival-ride slider that corkscrews in on lefties is a major league-quality weapon when it stays on the tracks. Despite the more extensive work, his peripherals are mostly trending in the right direction, except for that pesky home run rate. Given his career performance in the minors, it's likely the HR rate will regress, and with continued improvement in command, the Yak Attack should be able to stick on the 25-man, preferably as a late-inning option.

YEAR	TEAM	LVL	AGE	WHIP	ERA	DRA	WARP	MPH	FB%	WHF	CSP
2016	FRD	A+	24	1.13	3.98	3.64	0.3				
2016	BOW	AA	24	1.08	2.03	2.50	1.2				
2017	NOR	AAA	25	0.95	1.32	4.00	0.9				
2017	BAL	MLB	25	1.55	4.35	7.28	-0.5	96.9	72.9	6.2	46.4
2018	NOR	AAA	26	1.22	4.26	3.96	1.4				
2018	BAL	MLB	26	1.45	5.40	7.66	-1.1	95.1	62.8	10.8	47.3
2019	BAL	MLB	27	1.47	5.41	5.23	0.0	95.1	66.4	9.6	47.5

Jimmy Yacabonis, continued

Pitch Shape vs LHH

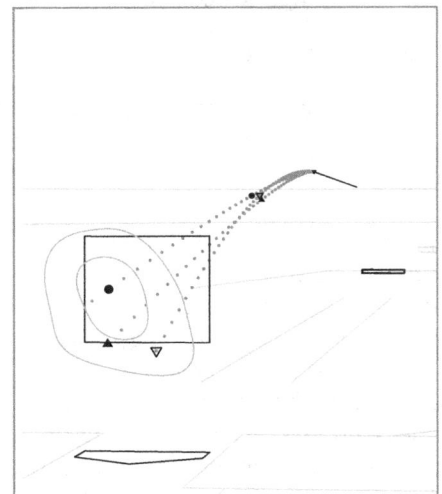

Pitch Shape vs RHH

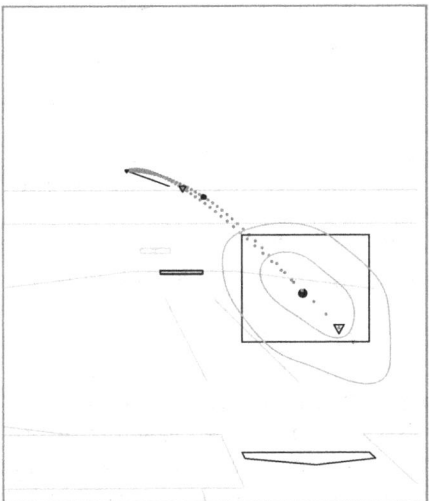

Type	Frequency	Velocity	H Movement	V Movement
● Fastball	62.8%	93.8 [104]	-14.7 [63]	-21 [83]
☐ Sinker				
+ Cutter				
▲ Changeup	5.5%	86.6 [105]	-13.1 [90]	-28.2 [97]
✕ Splitter				
▽ Slider	31.8%	83.5 [96]	8.9 [117]	-35.1 [94]
◇ Curveball				
⊕ Slow Curveball				
✱ Knuckleball				
▼ Screwball				

Orioles Player Analysis - 65

Rylan Bannon 2B

Born: 04/22/96 Age: 23 Bats: R Throws: R
Height: 5'10" Weight: 180 Origin: Round 8, 2017 Draft (#250 overall)

YEAR	TEAM	LVL	AGE	PA	R	2B	3B	HR	RBI	BB	K	SB	CS	AVG/OBP/SLG
2017	OGD	RK	21	175	39	8	0	10	30	19	29	5	0	.336/.425/.591
2018	RCU	A+	22	403	58	17	6	20	61	59	103	4	4	.296/.402/.559
2018	BOW	AA	22	122	16	6	0	2	11	22	24	0	0	.204/.344/.327
2019	BAL	MLB	23	251	30	8	1	9	27	30	70	0	0	.193/.290/.364

Breakout: 9% Improve: 26% Collapse: 5% Attrition: 15% MLB: 37%
Comparables: Vince Belnome, Adam Duvall, Brett Wallace

Bannon was being developed as a utility bat toward the end of his tenure with the Dodgers, but the Orioles could use his defensive ability at his natural home of third. Bannon isn't a typical light-hitting utilityman, though; the former Big East Player of the Year stormed into rookie ball, and the Dodgers aggressively promoted Bannon to High-A this season. The Orioles were even more aggressive, forwarding Bannon to Double-A Bowie, where his power predictably fell off over a hundred or so plate appearances, but the excellent plate discipline that's been a hallmark of his game since college remains intact. Something to monitor is whether the 5'10/180-lb Bannon can maintain his power numbers away from the hitter-friendly California League, but even if the power dips slightly, his profile is brimming with tools.

YEAR	TEAM	LVL	AGE	PA	DRC+	VORP	BABIP	BRR	FRAA	WARP
2017	OGD	RK	21	175	161	19.4	.360	0.8	3B(34): 5.9	1.9
2018	RCU	A+	22	403	161	35.8	.367	0.0	3B(54): 2.9, 2B(22): 0.2	2.9
2018	BOW	AA	22	122	100	2.5	.243	-1.4	2B(30): -0.9, 3B(2): -0.1	-0.1
2019	BAL	MLB	23	251	78	0.2	.233	-0.3	3B 1, 2B 0	0.1

Yusniel Diaz OF

Born: 10/07/96 Age: 22 Bats: R Throws: R
Height: 6'1" Weight: 195 Origin: International Free Agent, 2015

YEAR	TEAM	LVL	AGE	PA	R	2B	3B	HR	RBI	BB	K	SB	CS	AVG/OBP/SLG
2016	RCU	A+	19	348	47	8	7	8	54	29	71	7	8	.272/.333/.418
2017	RCU	A+	20	374	42	15	3	8	39	35	73	7	9	.278/.343/.414
2017	TUL	AA	20	118	15	8	0	3	13	10	29	2	5	.333/.390/.491
2018	TUL	AA	21	264	36	10	4	6	30	41	39	8	8	.314/.428/.477
2018	BOW	AA	21	152	23	5	1	5	15	18	28	4	5	.239/.329/.403
2019	BAL	MLB	22	251	25	7	1	7	27	16	64	3	3	.214/.264/.348

Breakout: 11% Improve: 35% Collapse: 1% Attrition: 21% MLB: 36%
Comparables: Domonic Brown, Billy McKinney, Caleb Gindl

The crown jewel of the Machado deal, Diaz—who immediately rocketed to the top of Orioles top prospect lists the moment he buttoned up his Bowie Baysox jersey—is close to major-league ready. Scouts wonder when or if his raw power will translate into game power, although he's seen a significant uptick in that area over the past two seasons. Diaz is a well-rounded player who is average-to-good in all categories, even if no one skill jumps off the page. He's a very good contact hitter with advanced plate discipline and has a strong enough arm to man right field even if he has to move off center, and while he may not fit the traditional power-bat model of a corner OF, his ability to barrel line drives to all fields while taking walks and limiting his strikeouts will be a tremendous boost to the team with the worst OBP in the AL in 2018. When he makes the majors, Diaz's plate appearances will be a balm upon the eyes of O's fans who watched Chris Davis strike out 36.8 percent of the time this season.

YEAR	TEAM	LVL	AGE	PA	DRC+	VORP	BABIP	BRR	FRAA	WARP
2016	RCU	A+	19	348	100	8.7	.326	-2.1	CF(34): -6.1, RF(15): -0.7	-0.9
2017	RCU	A+	20	374	96	8.9	.328	-1.0	CF(29): 1.8, RF(26): -1.2	-0.3
2017	TUL	AA	20	118	151	6.6	.434	-0.8	RF(26): -0.6, CF(5): -0.1	0.4
2018	TUL	AA	21	264	159	21.5	.360	1.8	CF(29): -1.7, RF(28): -1.6	1.5
2018	BOW	AA	21	152	97	4.6	.267	-0.5	RF(29): 0.3, CF(6): -0.5	-0.1
2019	BAL	MLB	22	251	60	-4.9	.259	-0.6	RF 0, CF -1	-0.7

Jean Carlos Encarnacion 3B

Born: 01/17/98   Age: 21   Bats: R   Throws: R
Height: 6'3"   Weight: 195   Origin: International Free Agent, 2016

YEAR	TEAM	LVL	AGE	PA	R	2B	3B	HR	RBI	BB	K	SB	CS	AVG/OBP/SLG
2016	DBR	RK	18	156	19	3	3	0	16	11	30	4	0	.264/.340/.329
2017	BRA	RK	19	107	16	8	4	2	16	4	22	4	2	.350/.374/.563
2017	DNV	RK	19	98	14	3	0	1	6	3	21	3	5	.290/.316/.355
2018	ROM	A	20	379	45	23	5	10	57	13	100	5	5	.288/.314/.463
2018	DEL	A	20	104	10	4	2	2	7	3	34	0	0	.218/.240/.356
2019	BAL	MLB	21	251	16	3	0	6	23	1	82	0	0	.170/.173/.258

Breakout: 5%   Improve: 8%   Collapse: 0%   Attrition: 8%   MLB: 8%
Comparables: Josh Bell, Nick Castellanos, Neftali Soto

One of four prospects obtained in the Gausman deal, the young, athletic Encarnacion is the kind of prospect the Braves have coming out of their ears and the Orioles...do not. Encarnacion's walk rate is nursery-rhyme puny, especially considering how often he strikes out, and he'll need to improve his plate discipline in order to tap into the raw power hidden in his 6'3" frame. He's shown flashes of it throughout his time in the low minors, and also a strong arm, fast-twitch muscles, and athletic ability that indicate he could stick at the hot corner if the Orioles are willing to take the time to work on the finer points of fielding with him, emphasis on *work*—Encarnacion had 30 errors at third in 92 games with the Rome Braves this season. Prospects with the kind of power upside Encarnacion possesses are few and far between in the Orioles system, and he'll play next season at just 21 years of age, so there's plenty of time for the Orioles to polish this particularly rough diamond.

YEAR	TEAM	LVL	AGE	PA	DRC+	VORP	BABIP	BRR	FRAA	WARP
2016	DBR	RK	18	156	100	6.5	.336	1.4	3B(19): -2.0, SS(16): 0.0	0.3
2017	BRA	RK	19	107	149	10.6	.430	0.3	3B(15): -1.9, 1B(14): 1.0	0.3
2017	DNV	RK	19	98	105	6.2	.361	0.9	3B(23): 4.1	0.6
2018	ROM	A	20	379	105	24.8	.370	-0.2	3B(92): 5.0	1.2
2018	DEL	A	20	104	106	2.6	.308	2.2	3B(21): 2.0	0.6
2019	BAL	MLB	21	251	6	-23.0	.224	-0.4	3B 2	-2.2

Cadyn Grenier SS
Born: 10/31/96 Age: 22 Bats: R Throws: R
Height: 5'11" Weight: 188 Origin: Round 1, 2018 Draft (#37 overall)

YEAR	TEAM	LVL	AGE	PA	R	2B	3B	HR	RBI	BB	K	SB	CS	AVG/OBP/SLG
2018	DEL	A	21	183	23	12	2	1	13	17	53	3	2	.216/.297/.333
2019	BAL	MLB	22	251	20	10	1	5	19	9	92	1	0	.149/.181/.257

Breakout: 4% Improve: 7% Collapse: 0% Attrition: 6% MLB: 8%
Comparables: Pete Kozma, Ian Desmond, Argenis Diaz

Two things about the Orioles' second overall pick in 2018: First, he lists his favorite movie as Ace Ventura 2: When Nature Calls. Not the first one; the sequel, and full title only, please. Second, although he names Troy Tulowitzki as his favorite player, Grenier also shares traits with fellow Vegas native Bryce Harper. Sporting similar hair and similar insouciant swag, Grenier plays short like Harper hits bombs, a relentless barrage of highlight reel plays that earned him a Pac-12 DPOY award over teammate, and fellow defensive wizard, Nick Madrigal. His challenge in pro ball will be to translate that swag to his offensive game, although he steadily improved in all offensive categories each year at Oregon State. Grenier's quick hands and ability to hit to all fields, plus reflexes of a cat and the speed of a mongoose, are a solid base to work from. Alrighty then!

YEAR	TEAM	LVL	AGE	PA	DRC+	VORP	BABIP	BRR	FRAA	WARP
2018	DEL	A	21	183	85	9.9	.312	-0.5	SS(39): 2.7	0.3
2019	BAL	MLB	22	251	16	-16.1	.212	-0.3	SS 2	-1.5

Baltimore Orioles 2019

Austin Hays OF
Born: 07/05/95   Age: 23   Bats: R   Throws: R
Height: 6'1"   Weight: 195   Origin: Round 3, 2016 Draft (#91 overall)

YEAR	TEAM	LVL	AGE	PA	R	2B	3B	HR	RBI	BB	K	SB	CS	AVG/OBP/SLG
2016	ABE	A-	20	153	14	9	2	4	21	11	32	4	3	.336/.386/.514
2017	FRD	A+	21	280	42	15	3	16	41	12	40	4	6	.328/.364/.592
2017	BOW	AA	21	283	39	17	2	16	54	13	45	1	1	.330/.367/.594
2017	BAL	MLB	21	63	4	3	0	1	8	2	16	0	0	.217/.238/.317
2018	BOW	AA	22	288	34	12	2	12	43	12	59	6	3	.242/.271/.432
2019	BAL	MLB	23	303	32	12	1	13	40	7	72	2	1	.237/.258/.419

Breakout: 15%   Improve: 44%   Collapse: 2%   Attrition: 22%   MLB: 54%
Comparables: Dayan Viciedo, Josh Kroeger, Anthony Santander

The O's have been aggressive with their 2016 third-rounder, going so far as to call him up to the majors in his first full season to help with a potential playoff push. Hays fell flat in his brief exposure to the majors and was summarily returned to Double-A Bowie last year, where he struggled over the first two months of the season before wrenching an ankle. He returned to Bowie in August and put together a strong conclusion to his season, with numbers much more in line with the totals he'd posted that earned him spots on various top prospect lists. The team had hoped to send him to the AFL to continue building on his strong finish and make up for lost time, but the ankle issue persisted, eventually requiring surgery. Hays should be ready for spring training, but there won't be another playoff run to compel the team to rush him a second time.

YEAR	TEAM	LVL	AGE	PA	DRC+	VORP	BABIP	BRR	FRAA	WARP
2016	ABE	A-	20	153	171	15.7	.410	-0.9	RF(20): 0.3, CF(5): 0.1	1.0
2017	FRD	A+	21	280	147	26.0	.337	0.7	CF(57): 8.1, RF(4): -0.6	2.5
2017	BOW	AA	21	283	152	31.3	.345	3.2	CF(32): -3.3, RF(29): -0.4	1.7
2017	BAL	MLB	21	63	70	-3.2	.273	-0.4	RF(14): -1.6, CF(8): -1.3	-0.4
2018	BOW	AA	22	288	89	8.3	.263	0.9	RF(36): 6.7, LF(16): -0.3	0.6
2019	BAL	MLB	23	303	77	0.2	.270	-0.4	RF 0, LF 0	-0.1

Ryan McKenna CF

Born: 02/14/97 Age: 22 Bats: R Throws: R
Height: 5'11" Weight: 185 Origin: Round 4, 2015 Draft (#133 overall)

YEAR	TEAM	LVL	AGE	PA	R	2B	3B	HR	RBI	BB	K	SB	CS	AVG/OBP/SLG
2016	ABE	A-	19	252	29	10	1	1	26	22	59	17	6	.241/.320/.309
2017	DEL	A	20	530	62	33	2	7	42	43	128	20	2	.256/.331/.380
2018	FRD	A+	21	301	60	18	2	8	37	37	45	5	6	.377/.467/.556
2018	BOW	AA	21	250	35	8	2	3	16	29	56	4	1	.239/.341/.338
2019	BAL	MLB	22	251	26	8	1	6	22	16	69	2	1	.200/.260/.318

Breakout: 17% Improve: 44% Collapse: 0% Attrition: 18% MLB: 47%
Comparables: Delino DeShields, Ryan Kalish, Andrew McCutchen

Moss campion, also called the compass plant, is a hardy wildflower that is able to tolerate a harsh Arctic climate by creating a dense interior space that is warm and sheltered from the wind, a mini-nursery that will issue shocking pink blooms in the summer. Like the moss campion, Maine native Ryan McKenna has been a slow-growing perennial since being drafted in 2015, but exploded in dazzling color this summer for High-A Frederick. Improved plate discipline, especially a better two-strike approach, has unlocked the potential in McKenna's bat, as have some mechanical refinements, such as adding a toe tap. While his frame doesn't foreshadow a lot of balls over the fence, McKenna can spray line drives all over the field and is quick enough to nab an extra base here and there. That speed also helps him in center, where his arm is graded by most scouts as average, to occasionally make a highlight-reel diving catch. After a promotion to Double-A, the Orioles assigned McKenna to the AFL, a somewhat more hospitable environment to which the former cold-weather prospect has quickly adapted.

YEAR	TEAM	LVL	AGE	PA	DRC+	VORP	BABIP	BRR	FRAA	WARP
2016	ABE	A-	19	252	103	8.0	.319	1.5	CF(57): 0.5	0.4
2017	DEL	A	20	530	116	29.0	.336	-0.2	CF(124): -7.6	0.9
2018	FRD	A+	21	301	210	46.2	.436	2.5	CF(64): -6.2, LF(2): -0.2	3.4
2018	BOW	AA	21	250	91	10.6	.312	2.6	CF(55): 3.4, RF(3): 2.1	0.9
2019	BAL	MLB	22	251	59	-3.2	.255	-0.2	CF -1, LF 0	-0.5

Ryan Mountcastle 3B

Born: 02/18/97 Age: 22 Bats: R Throws: R
Height: 6'3" Weight: 195 Origin: Round 1, 2015 Draft (#36 overall)

YEAR	TEAM	LVL	AGE	PA	R	2B	3B	HR	RBI	BB	K	SB	CS	AVG/OBP/SLG
2016	DEL	A	19	489	53	28	4	10	51	25	95	5	4	.281/.319/.426
2017	FRD	A+	20	379	63	35	1	15	47	14	61	8	2	.314/.343/.542
2017	BOW	AA	20	159	18	13	0	3	15	3	35	0	0	.222/.239/.366
2018	BOW	AA	21	428	63	19	4	13	59	26	79	2	0	.297/.341/.464
2019	BAL	MLB	22	251	22	12	1	8	29	5	61	0	0	.224/.240/.376

Breakout: 16% Improve: 30% Collapse: 6% Attrition: 25% MLB: 36%
Comparables: Josh Vitters, Brandon Laird, Renato Nunez

The Orioles have been stockpiling bat-first prospects and Mountcastle, a compensation pick for losing Nelson Cruz in 2015, is no exception. The team gave up on the illusion of Mountcastle playing shortstop this year, moving him to third, but many scouts see his eventual defensive home in left field. That adds to a logjam of bat-first, defensively-limited prospects in the O's system; with Mountcastle being one of the youngest of these, and not needing protection on the 40-man yet, look for him to spend time ripening in the minors as the O's sort out their major-league situation. If he can stick at third, that will accelerate the timeline significantly. Mountcastle has made an obvious attempt to take more walks and turned in a strong season at Double-A thanks to his ability to hit for average, but he'll need to maintain that selectivity at the plate to push his power numbers up if he wants to be the Mount in the high castle of Camden Yards.

YEAR	TEAM	LVL	AGE	PA	DRC+	VORP	BABIP	BRR	FRAA	WARP
2016	DEL	A	19	489	111	25.2	.331	-1.7	SS(105): -21.1	-1.0
2017	FRD	A+	20	379	135	28.9	.343	1.5	SS(82): -12.1	1.1
2017	BOW	AA	20	159	57	-0.4	.265	0.5	3B(37): -1.1	-0.6
2018	BOW	AA	21	428	117	22.2	.339	-1.5	3B(81): -4.9	0.8
2019	BAL	MLB	22	251	63	-5.8	.265	-0.3	3B -3	-0.9

Rio Ruiz 3B

Born: 05/22/94 Age: 25 Bats: L Throws: R
Height: 6'1" Weight: 215 Origin: Round 4, 2012 Draft (#129 overall)

YEAR	TEAM	LVL	AGE	PA	R	2B	3B	HR	RBI	BB	K	SB	CS	AVG/OBP/SLG
2016	GWN	AAA	22	533	52	24	3	10	62	61	116	1	4	.271/.355/.400
2016	ATL	MLB	22	7	1	0	1	0	2	0	2	1	0	.286/.286/.571
2017	GWN	AAA	23	432	48	25	2	16	56	42	110	1	2	.247/.322/.446
2017	ATL	MLB	23	173	22	5	0	4	19	19	41	1	0	.193/.283/.307
2018	GWN	AAA	24	541	72	25	4	9	72	40	90	2	1	.269/.322/.390
2018	ATL	MLB	24	15	1	0	0	0	0	2	5	0	0	.083/.267/.083
2019	BAL	MLB	25	70	7	3	0	2	8	6	17	0	0	.219/.286/.359

Breakout: 8% Improve: 34% Collapse: 1% Attrition: 30% MLB: 52%
Comparables: Max Muncy, Colin Moran, Brian Anderson

Ruiz was never considered a real option as the next long-term third baseman in Atlanta, but it's to the point now that he needs to start doing something in the majors to avoid the Quad-A label. He hasn't done much other than walk in his two short stints in the majors and he's fallen behind on the depth chart as younger whippersnappers make their moves. The realistic role was always something along the lines of a left-handed bench option with plate discipline as the main strength, while the ceiling was a platoon mate. He still has time to revive that, but someone is on call to perform CPR at a moment's notice.

YEAR	TEAM	LVL	AGE	PA	DRC+	VORP	BABIP	BRR	FRAA	WARP
2016	GWN	AAA	22	533	109	14.8	.337	-3.8	3B(119): -7.0	0.4
2016	ATL	MLB	22	7	75	0.3	.400	0.2	3B(2): -0.1	0.0
2017	GWN	AAA	23	432	114	13.9	.304	-0.2	3B(91): 2.0, 1B(5): 0.2	1.6
2017	ATL	MLB	23	173	76	-0.9	.231	0.9	3B(41): 0.6, 1B(2): 0.0	0.3
2018	GWN	AAA	24	541	96	9.9	.311	1.8	3B(49): 2.3, 1B(35): 1.5	0.4
2018	ATL	MLB	24	15	78	0.3	.143	-0.1	3B(1): -0.2	0.0
2019	BAL	MLB	25	70	65	-1.4	.265	-0.1	3B 0	-0.2

D.J. Stewart OF

Born: 11/30/93 Age: 25 Bats: L Throws: R
Height: 6'0" Weight: 230 Origin: Round 1, 2015 Draft (#25 overall)

YEAR	TEAM	LVL	AGE	PA	R	2B	3B	HR	RBI	BB	K	SB	CS	AVG/OBP/SLG
2016	DEL	A	22	262	27	12	1	4	25	42	58	16	6	.230/.366/.352
2016	FRD	A+	22	240	41	12	2	6	30	36	46	10	3	.279/.389/.448
2017	BOW	AA	23	540	80	26	2	21	79	65	87	20	4	.278/.378/.481
2018	NOR	AAA	24	490	59	24	2	12	55	54	103	11	4	.235/.329/.387
2018	BAL	MLB	24	47	8	3	0	3	10	4	12	2	1	.250/.340/.550
2019	BAL	MLB	25	280	33	11	1	9	30	25	64	6	2	.209/.289/.369

Breakout: 8%   Improve: 24%   Collapse: 4%   Attrition: 26%   MLB: 42%
Comparables: Bronson Sardinha, Thomas Neal, Phil Ervin

In 2017, Stewart changed his stance from "Albert Pujols with the Duomo strapped to his back" and, after a year of realigning his spine, had his most successful season as a pro. The former first-round pick didn't have quite as much success this season at Triple-A, where his strikeouts surged and his offense fell off across the board, but that didn't stop the Orioles from giving him a taste of MLB action. In just under 50 PAs, Stewart went deep three times, with three doubles, hinting that the bat will play in the majors. He also swiped two bags, reinforcing his reputation as an excellent base-runner. Unfortunately, like Mancini, the defensively-limited Stewart is marooned between the Scylla and Charybdis of Mark Trumbo and Chris Davis, so he might have to hang out and chew some lotus until the way forward reveals itself.

YEAR	TEAM	LVL	AGE	PA	DRC+	VORP	BABIP	BRR	FRAA	WARP
2016	DEL	A	22	262	123	7.3	.294	-1.2	LF(58): 0.2	0.6
2016	FRD	A+	22	240	121	10.7	.333	0.0	LF(51): 1.0, CF(2): -0.2	0.5
2017	BOW	AA	23	540	132	37.6	.299	2.1	LF(113): -0.6, RF(4): 0.7	2.3
2018	NOR	AAA	24	490	105	14.4	.278	4.7	RF(88): -14.1, LF(24): 1.9	-0.2
2018	BAL	MLB	24	47	88	3.2	.269	0.5	LF(9): 4.4, RF(6): -0.4	0.5
2019	BAL	MLB	25	280	77	-0.1	.242	0.3	RF -4, LF 1	-0.4

Engelb Vielma   INF

Born: 06/22/94   Age: 25   Bats: B   Throws: R
Height: 5'11"   Weight: 155   Origin: International Free Agent, 2011

YEAR	TEAM	LVL	AGE	PA	R	2B	3B	HR	RBI	BB	K	SB	CS	AVG/OBP/SLG
2016	FTM	A+	22	30	5	0	0	0	0	5	8	2	0	.200/.333/.200
2016	CHT	AA	22	367	47	7	4	0	21	34	62	10	8	.271/.345/.318
2017	CHT	AA	23	141	7	5	0	0	18	14	13	1	3	.286/.362/.328
2017	ROC	AAA	23	314	36	12	2	0	17	11	72	2	5	.206/.233/.260
2018	BAL	MLB	24	8	1	0	0	0	0	1	4	0	0	.143/.250/.143
2018	NOR	AAA	24	43	3	2	1	0	3	4	9	0	0	.184/.256/.289
2019	BAL	MLB	25	251	22	6	1	4	21	12	57	2	2	.217/.259/.303

Breakout: 15%   Improve: 26%   Collapse: 0%   Attrition: 18%   MLB: 26%
Comparables: Andrew Romine, Rafael Ynoa, Mike Freeman

Whatever kind of a stinker you feel you've been handed in the last name derby, we feel confident in suggesting it's better than the lot that befell one Engelb Stalin Vielma. That's "Engelb," like someone got partway through writing "Engelbert" and got bored; "Stalin," like Stalin; and "Vielma," which would probably be fine on its own but in concert with the rest of the name summons images of food-borne parasites, Scooby-Doo characters, and/or mechanically reclaimed meat. All that said, thank goodness Vielma played for the 2018 Baltimore Orioles, for while the name Engelb Vielma is 80-grade, nothing else about the player is, and on a more competent team, the baseball record books might have been denied this glory.

YEAR	TEAM	LVL	AGE	PA	DRC+	VORP	BABIP	BRR	FRAA	WARP
2016	FTM	A+	22	30	85	0.1	.294	-0.6	SS(4): 0.9, 2B(3): -0.5	0.0
2016	CHT	AA	22	367	99	12.1	.333	1.6	SS(57): -0.1, 3B(21): 2.8	1.0
2017	CHT	AA	23	141	122	5.2	.312	-1.3	SS(19): -0.2, 2B(14): 0.2	0.4
2017	ROC	AAA	23	314	33	-1.6	.266	3.2	SS(84): 3.8, 2B(2): -0.3	-0.6
2018	BAL	MLB	24	8	70	0.5	.333	1.0	2B(4): -0.3, SS(2): 0.0	0.1
2018	NOR	AAA	24	43	55	-0.2	.233	0.3	SS(12): 0.0	0.0
2019	BAL	MLB	25	251	48	-6.9	.264	-0.3	SS 1, 2B 0	-0.5

Keegan Akin   LHP

Born: 04/01/95   Age: 24   Bats: L   Throws: L
Height: 6'0"   Weight: 225   Origin: Round 2, 2016 Draft (#54 overall)

YEAR	TEAM	LVL	AGE	W	L	SV	G	GS	IP	H	HR	BB/9	K/9	K	GB%	BABIP
2016	ABE	A-	21	0	1	0	9	9	26	15	0	2.4	10.0	29	51%	.231
2017	FRD	A+	22	7	8	0	21	21	100	89	12	4.1	10.0	111	38%	.307
2018	BOW	AA	23	14	7	0	25	25	137[2]	114	16	3.8	9.3	142	32%	.278
2019	BAL	MLB	24	5	9	0	22	22	106[1]	109	21	4.2	8.5	100	35%	.297

Breakout: 6%   Improve: 11%   Collapse: 5%   Attrition: 12%   MLB: 19%
Comparables: Caleb Smith, James Houser, Drew Anderson

Listed at six feet tall, Akin's stuff plays like he's much taller, thanks to the sharp downward plane the stocky lefty is able to generate with his mechanics. Akin has three solid pitches in a low-to-mid 90s fastball, a slider with some sharp movement, and a changeup that will make the difference as to whether he's a back-of-the-rotation piece or a Quad-A/swingman type. The Western Michigan grad has made steady progress through the system since being drafted in 2016 and shown an ability to miss bats at every level, including an impressive AFL stint in 2017. An oblique injury slowed him last season, but he returned to full health this year and posted one of the strongest seasons for a starting pitcher in the Eastern League. Akin won the Eastern League Pitcher of the Year Award with Double-A Bowie, the first time an Orioles pitcher has won the award in a decade.

YEAR	TEAM	LVL	AGE	WHIP	ERA	DRA	WARP	MPH	FB%	WHF	CSP
2016	ABE	A-	21	0.85	1.04	4.46	0.2				
2017	FRD	A+	22	1.35	4.14	5.88	-0.7				
2018	BOW	AA	23	1.25	3.27	4.07	2.0				
2019	BAL	MLB	24	1.50	5.58	5.51	0.0				

Cameron Bishop LHP

Born: 02/14/96 Age: 23 Bats: L Throws: L
Height: 6'4" Weight: 215 Origin: Round 26, 2017 Draft (#788 overall)

YEAR	TEAM	LVL	AGE	W	L	SV	G	GS	IP	H	HR	BB/9	K/9	K	GB%	BABIP
2017	ABE	A-	21	1	1	0	8	8	34^2	20	1	4.2	9.9	38	51%	.232
2018	DEL	A	22	9	7	0	22	22	125^2	107	5	1.4	7.1	99	50%	.274
2019	BAL	MLB	23	3	7	0	16	16	83	97	15	3.6	6.1	56	42%	.305

Breakout: 2%   Improve: 2%   Collapse: 4%   Attrition: 5%   MLB: 7%
Comparables: Jason Adam, Ryan Sherriff, Trevor Williams

The Orioles almost Orioles'd themselves out of Bishop's services by submitting his draft paperwork late, but the kind overlords of MLB took pity on Bishop, if being drafted by the Orioles qualifies as being pitied. A strained oblique cost Bishop his junior year of college and subsequently his draft standing, but Baltimore, sensing a deal, took the big lefty in the 26th round and signed him well overslot. The Orioles built Bishop's innings slowly through 2017 and continued a middle-of-the-road approach in 2018, assigning him to Single-A Delmarva. For the Shorebirds, Bishop proved to be a durable, reliable starter who doesn't record eye-popping strikeout numbers but also doesn't walk anyone, elicits plenty of ground balls, and keeps the ball in the yard. Bishop has a simple, repeatable delivery out of a high overhand slot with some sharp downward plane action. Bishop also throws a slider, curve, and changeup, all of which need significant refinement before they are major-league quality pitches.

YEAR	TEAM	LVL	AGE	WHIP	ERA	DRA	WARP	MPH	FB%	WHF	CSP
2017	ABE	A-	21	1.04	0.78	3.11	0.9				
2018	DEL	A	22	1.01	2.94	3.71	2.2				
2019	BAL	MLB	23	1.57	5.85	5.77	-0.3				

Baltimore Orioles 2019

DL Hall LHP
Born: 09/19/98   Age: 20   Bats: L   Throws: L
Height: 6'2"   Weight: 195   Origin: Round 1, 2017 Draft (#21 overall)

YEAR	TEAM	LVL	AGE	W	L	SV	G	GS	IP	H	HR	BB/9	K/9	K	GB%	BABIP
2017	ORI	RK	18	0	0	0	5	5	10^1	10	1	8.7	10.5	12	58%	.360
2018	DEL	A	19	2	7	0	22	20	94^1	68	6	4.0	9.5	100	46%	.262
2019	BAL	MLB	20	2	7	0	14	14	57^2	62	11	7.6	8.1	52	44%	.304

Breakout: 2%   Improve: 2%   Collapse: 1%   Attrition: 3%   MLB: 4%
Comparables: Josh Hader, Sean Gallagher, Jeurys Familia

Let you love anything like Baltimore loves taking a prep pitcher in the first round. Baltimore's 2017 first-rounder (#21 overall) garners high praise for his late-breaking power curve, especially effective out of a deceptive left-handed slot, and his mid-90s fastball gives him the floor of a back-end bullpen arm, although of course the Orioles are hoping for more. After a strong full first year of pro ball at Single-A, Hall's ceiling looks much higher than that, provided he can polish a third pitch and tweak his delivery to land more pitches in the strike zone. In the meantime, his ability to put batters away with either the fastball or the deadly curve should propel Hall onto some top-100 lists in the near future. Love what you love, kittens.

YEAR	TEAM	LVL	AGE	WHIP	ERA	DRA	WARP	MPH	FB%	WHF	CSP
2017	ORI	RK	18	1.94	6.97	4.79	0.1				
2018	DEL	A	19	1.17	2.10	3.69	1.7				
2019	BAL	MLB	20	1.91	6.87	6.85	-0.9				

Brenan Hanifee   RHP

Born: 05/29/98   Age: 21   Bats: R   Throws: R
Height: 6'5"   Weight: 180   Origin: Round 4, 2016 Draft (#121 overall)

YEAR	TEAM	LVL	AGE	W	L	SV	G	GS	IP	H	HR	BB/9	K/9	K	GB%	BABIP
2017	ABE	A-	19	7	3	0	12	12	68^2	65	2	1.6	5.8	44	59%	.289
2018	DEL	A	20	8	6	0	23	23	132	120	8	1.5	5.8	85	55%	.275
2019	BAL	MLB	21	4	8	0	16	16	92	113	16	2.9	4.6	47	48%	.304

Breakout: 6%   Improve: 7%   Collapse: 1%   Attrition: 1%   MLB: 8%
Comparables: Alex Cobb, Kohl Stewart, Jair Jurrjens

Hanifee grew up playing baseball on a field his father built in Northern Virginia, and spent 2018 playing for the Delmarva Shorebirds, just over four hours from his hometown. Hanifee was listed at 6'5"/185 when he was drafted out of high school in 2016, and it doesn't look like he's added much bulk to his frame since. A back injury has forced the Orioles to build his innings slowly, but when he's been on the mound the results have been solid. So far, Hanifee doesn't miss many bats, but he also doesn't walk batters, and he's able to generate a high number of groundball outs and keep the ball in the park with a fastball that, despite below-average velocity, has plenty of armside run and sink. That's an appealing profile for any pitcher, but especially one based in the AL East.

YEAR	TEAM	LVL	AGE	WHIP	ERA	DRA	WARP	MPH	FB%	WHF	CSP
2017	ABE	A-	19	1.12	2.75	3.57	1.4				
2018	DEL	A	20	1.08	2.86	3.91	2.0				
2019	BAL	MLB	21	1.55	5.85	5.76	-0.3				

Hunter Harvey RHP

Born: 12/09/94 Age: 24 Bats: R Throws: R
Height: 6'3" Weight: 175 Origin: Round 1, 2013 Draft (#22 overall)

YEAR	TEAM	LVL	AGE	W	L	SV	G	GS	IP	H	HR	BB/9	K/9	K	GB%	BABIP
2017	DEL	A	22	0	1	0	3	3	8²	4	0	3.1	14.5	14	31%	.250
2018	BOW	AA	23	1	2	0	9	9	32¹	36	3	2.5	8.4	30	36%	.351
2019	BAL	MLB	24	1	2	0	5	5	26	28	6	4.3	8.0	24	37%	.296

Breakout: 3%   Improve: 7%   Collapse: 4%   Attrition: 9%   MLB: 14%
Comparables: Daniel Poncedeleon, Rob Rasmussen, Spencer Turnbull

When risk-averse front office execs give presentations about Why Picking High School Pitchers in the First Round is Bad, the first slide is a picture of Harvey. Five years after being drafted 22nd overall by the O's, Harvey has yet to throw a pitch above Double-A. His injuries have been of both the typical baseball pitcher variety, including a flexor mass strain and Tommy John surgery in 2016, and of the freakish bad luck variety, including a fractured fibula after being drilled by a line drive during Spring Training in 2015 and popping his shoulder trying to dodge a foul ball in the dugout. When he's been on the field, Harvey has posted strong results against low-level hitters. The team had to add Harvey to the 40-man this past off-season to protect him against the Rule 5 Draft, so if he holds it together against the upper minors early next season, expect pitching-starved Baltimore to be aggressive in promoting Harvey, as long as he's relatively whole.

YEAR	TEAM	LVL	AGE	WHIP	ERA	DRA	WARP	MPH	FB%	WHF	CSP
2017	DEL	A	22	0.81	2.08	2.57	0.3				
2018	BOW	AA	23	1.39	5.57	4.17	0.4				
2019	BAL	MLB	24	1.57	5.79	5.83	-0.1				

Nate Karns   RHP

Born: 11/25/87   Age: 31   Bats: R   Throws: R
Height: 6'3"   Weight: 225   Origin: Round 12, 2009 Draft (#352 overall)

YEAR	TEAM	LVL	AGE	W	L	SV	G	GS	IP	H	HR	BB/9	K/9	K	GB%	BABIP
2016	SEA	MLB	28	6	2	1	22	15	94^1	95	11	4.3	9.6	101	43%	.327
2017	KCA	MLB	29	2	2	0	9	8	45^1	41	9	2.6	10.1	51	48%	.283
2019	BAL	MLB	31	3	5	0	36	8	69	64	9	3.8	9.2	71	44%	.294

Breakout: 29%   Improve: 52%   Collapse: 20%   Attrition: 20%   MLB: 87%
Comparables: Chris Narveson, Matt Shoemaker, Tom Gorzelanny

Karns last threw a competitive pitch on May 19, 2017, when Brian Dozier flied out to center to end the bottom of the fifth. That otherwise unremarkable at-bat only gains significance as it recedes in the rear-view mirror, with only pain, surgery, rehab and waiting filling the space between. After missing most of 2017 and all of 2018 with thoracic outlet surgery, Karns enters 2019 hoping that a random Friday night in May represents the end of a chapter rather than the end of a career.

YEAR	TEAM	LVL	AGE	WHIP	ERA	DRA	WARP	MPH	FB%	WHF	CSP
2016	SEA	MLB	28	1.48	5.15	4.50	0.9	95.8	52.8	11.6	48.2
2017	KCA	MLB	29	1.19	4.17	4.94	0.3	95.1	49.4	13.6	47.7
2019	BAL	MLB	31	1.35	4.24	4.21	0.9	94.7	51.2	12.3	47.6

Baltimore Orioles 2019

Blaine Knight   RHP
Born: 06/28/96   Age: 23   Bats: R   Throws: R
Height: 6'3"   Weight: 165   Origin: Round 3, 2018 Draft (#87 overall)

YEAR	TEAM	LVL	AGE	W	L	SV	G	GS	IP	H	HR	BB/9	K/9	K	GB%	BABIP
2018	ABE	A-	22	0	1	0	4	4	10^1	13	1	2.6	7.0	8	34%	.353
2019	BAL	MLB	23	1	4	0	7	7	31^1	41	8	4.3	5.3	18	32%	.314

Breakout: 1%   Improve: 1%   Collapse: 0%   Attrition: 0%   MLB: 1%
Comparables: Joseph Mantiply, Tanner Rainey, Dillon Peters

A 2018 draftee out of Arkansas, Knight went undefeated during the regular season and carried the Razorbacks into the postseason. After a heavy innings workload, he was soft-pedaled in his first summer of pro ball, tossing just 10 innings at short-season Aberdeen. When he's up to speed, the polished Knight should move quickly through the O's system thanks to his poise on the mound and plus command of a dynamic four-pitch mix, including a 91-95 mph fastball that can touch 97, a plus slider, and a passable curveball and changeup. Durability questions have dogged the slightly-built Knight since college, but a major-league conditioning program should help Knight add some good muscle to his 6'3"/170-pound frame. And even if he doesn't, being slight hasn't hurt Chris Sale (6'6"/180), Blake Snell (6'5"/180), Jacob DeGrom (6'4"/180), or Kyle Freeland (6'3"/170).

YEAR	TEAM	LVL	AGE	WHIP	ERA	DRA	WARP	MPH	FB%	WHF	CSP
2018	ABE	A-	22	1.55	2.61	2.75	0.3				
2019	BAL	MLB	23	1.79	7.20	7.16	-0.6				

Dean Kremer   RHP

Born: 01/07/96 Age: 23 Bats: R Throws: R
Height: 6'3" Weight: 180 Origin: Round 14, 2016 Draft (#431 overall)

YEAR	TEAM	LVL	AGE	W	L	SV	G	GS	IP	H	HR	BB/9	K/9	K	GB%	BABIP
2016	OGD	RK	20	0	1	0	6	6	16¹	15	0	1.7	7.2	13	46%	.312
2016	GRL	A	20	2	0	0	6	0	15¹	4	0	2.3	12.9	22	52%	.148
2017	RCU	A+	21	1	4	3	33	6	80	86	6	3.8	10.8	96	43%	.369
2018	RCU	A+	22	5	3	0	16	16	79	67	7	3.0	13.0	114	40%	.351
2018	TUL	AA	22	1	0	0	1	1	7	3	0	3.9	14.1	11	75%	.250
2018	BOW	AA	22	4	2	0	8	8	45¹	38	3	3.4	10.5	53	41%	.310
2019	BAL	MLB	23	5	6	1	43	15	99¹	95	13	4.0	9.8	108	41%	.311

Breakout: 8% Improve: 14% Collapse: 9% Attrition: 18% MLB: 31%
Comparables: Tanner Roark, Vincent Velasquez, Michael Blazek

If Yusniel Diaz headlined the Machado trade, Kremer neck-lined it. Or possibly stomach-lined it, depending on if his future is truly as a back-end starter or, as some scouts seem inclined to believe, a bullpen piece. Kremer has a four-pitch mix with two MLB-ready offerings: a slow, loopy curveball that induces lots of whiffs, and a fastball that is effective despite average velocity, perhaps as a result of an elite spin rate. Even the homer-happy California League couldn't depress his strong numbers, and Kremer's one game in the Texas League was a sterling performance before he was sent to the Eastern League. The velocity-loving Dodgers didn't have much use for a soft-tossing prospect, but Baltimore can't afford to be as picky, so the move to the Orioles' system might be Kremer's best chance to make that starter money in his baseball career. Notable: Kremer was the first Israeli drafted by a Major League Baseball team and a member of the memorable Team Israel in the 2017 World Baseball Classic.

YEAR	TEAM	LVL	AGE	WHIP	ERA	DRA	WARP	MPH	FB%	WHF	CSP
2016	OGD	RK	20	1.10	3.86	3.60	0.4				
2016	GRL	A	20	0.52	0.59	2.48	0.4				
2017	RCU	A+	21	1.50	5.18	3.90	1.0				
2018	RCU	A+	22	1.18	3.30	3.38	1.8				
2018	TUL	AA	22	0.86	0.00	1.84	0.3				
2018	BOW	AA	22	1.21	2.58	3.61	0.9				
2019	BAL	MLB	23	1.41	4.41	4.28	1.5				

Zac Lowther LHP

Born: 04/30/96 Age: 23 Bats: L Throws: L
Height: 6'2" Weight: 235 Origin: Round 2, 2017 Draft (#74 overall)

YEAR	TEAM	LVL	AGE	W	L	SV	G	GS	IP	H	HR	BB/9	K/9	K	GB%	BABIP
2017	ABE	A-	21	2	2	0	12	11	54^1	35	1	1.8	12.4	75	47%	.283
2018	DEL	A	22	3	1	0	6	6	31	12	2	2.6	14.8	51	33%	.192
2018	FRD	A+	22	5	3	0	17	16	92^2	74	6	2.5	9.7	100	40%	.288
2019	BAL	MLB	23	4	7	0	17	17	87^1	85	14	3.4	9.3	90	37%	.301

Breakout: 3% Improve: 6% Collapse: 15% Attrition: 17% MLB: 25%
Comparables: Aaron Blair, Jon Gray, Dylan Bundy

If Lowther were a cheese, he'd be one of those cheeses carried only by specialty cheesemongers, with a lengthy handwritten card extolling his virtues and recommending you buy now, pay no attention to those ratings in Cheese Fancier Magazine that see only a low-level pitcher with a below-average fastball. After a strong pro debut after being drafted in the competitive balance round in 2017, Lowther plowed into Single-A Delmarva intent on splitting it back into three distinct states. After six dominant starts, the Orioles gleefully promoted Lowther to High-A Frederick, where he saw his strikeouts drop, but held his other peripherals in check. (A "drop" in strikeouts for Lowther meant that he went from striking out 44 percent of batters to a mere 27 percent. Yawn.) What makes the lanky, leggy lefty so difficult isn't the velocity on his fastball, but a highly deceptive delivery, with lots of whip and extension and funk. Zac Lowther, the Funky Cheese Man; you're welcome in advance, Orioles marketing department.

YEAR	TEAM	LVL	AGE	WHIP	ERA	DRA	WARP	MPH	FB%	WHF	CSP
2017	ABE	A-	21	0.85	1.66	2.59	1.7				
2018	DEL	A	22	0.68	1.16	2.38	1.0				
2018	FRD	A+	22	1.08	2.53	3.88	1.5				
2019	BAL	MLB	23	1.35	4.65	4.53	1.0				

Luis Ortiz RHP

Born: 09/22/95 Age: 23 Bats: R Throws: R
Height: 6'3" Weight: 230 Origin: Round 1, 2014 Draft (#30 overall)

YEAR	TEAM	LVL	AGE	W	L	SV	G	GS	IP	H	HR	BB/9	K/9	K	GB%	BABIP
2016	HDS	A+	20	3	2	0	7	6	27²	23	4	2.0	9.1	28	51%	.264
2016	FRI	AA	20	1	4	1	9	8	39²	47	3	1.6	7.7	34	47%	.352
2016	BLX	AA	20	2	2	0	6	6	23¹	26	2	3.9	6.2	16	33%	.316
2017	BLX	AA	21	4	7	0	22	20	94¹	79	12	3.5	7.5	79	36%	.258
2018	BLX	AA	22	3	4	2	16	11	68	63	7	2.4	8.6	65	48%	.289
2018	NOR	AAA	22	2	1	0	6	6	31²	34	4	2.3	6.0	21	40%	.297
2018	BAL	MLB	22	0	1	0	2	1	2¹	7	0	11.6	0.0	0	53%	.467
2019	BAL	MLB	23	2	3	0	16	5	38¹	40	6	3.3	7.1	30	41%	.294

Breakout: 11% Improve: 15% Collapse: 13% Attrition: 28% MLB: 34%
Comparables: Taylor Guerrieri, Alex Cobb, Ronald Herrera

Ortiz has now been the centerpiece of two high-profile trades, first acquired by the Brewers from the Rangers in the Jonathan Lucroy trade, and then flipped in the Jonathan Schoop trade. A hearty serving of a fellow at 6'3" and 230 pounds, Ortiz has been able to rely on overpowering minor-league hitters with pure velocity mixed with a nasty slider, but his production has become uneven as he's moved up into the high minors, and his cup of coffee in the majors was short and bitter. A recurrent hamstring injury has also slowed his progress, and scouting reports are filled with vague references to "conditioning," which is scout-speak for "likely candidate to slip on an empty bag of potato chips and throw out his back." His ability to throw strikes means Ortiz has an absolute floor of a back-end reliever, but the O's are counting on getting at least a back-end starter out of him.

YEAR	TEAM	LVL	AGE	WHIP	ERA	DRA	WARP	MPH	FB%	WHF	CSP
2016	HDS	A+	20	1.05	2.60	3.19	0.7				
2016	FRI	AA	20	1.36	4.08	4.10	0.5				
2016	BLX	AA	20	1.54	1.93	3.41	0.5				
2017	BLX	AA	21	1.23	4.01	3.43	1.9				
2018	BLX	AA	22	1.19	3.71	3.49	1.4				
2018	NOR	AAA	22	1.33	3.69	7.37	-0.6				
2018	BAL	MLB	22	4.29	15.43	7.94	-0.1	94.0	59.1	9.1	41.8
2019	BAL	MLB	23	1.42	5.08	4.96	0.2	93.9	61.2	9.4	43.3

Zach Pop   RHP

Born: 09/20/96   Age: 22   Bats: R   Throws: R
Height: 6'4"   Weight: 220   Origin: Round 7, 2017 Draft (#220 overall)

YEAR	TEAM	LVL	AGE	W	L	SV	G	GS	IP	H	HR	BB/9	K/9	K	GB%	BABIP
2018	GRL	A	21	0	2	0	11	0	16¹	12	1	3.9	13.2	24	60%	.297
2018	RCU	A+	21	1	0	7	19	0	27	13	0	2.0	7.7	23	68%	.197
2018	BOW	AA	21	1	1	1	14	0	21¹	14	0	2.5	7.2	17	70%	.246
2019	BAL	MLB	22	2	1	1	37	0	39	38	5	5.7	8.1	35	52%	.297

Breakout: 18%   Improve: 21%   Collapse: 1%   Attrition: 3%   MLB: 22%
Comparables: Dominic Leone, Jake Barrett, Trevor Gott

Besides having a name that sounds like a zippy 1950s soda, Pop made a good impression on his new team when he came over from the Dodgers in the Machado trade, basically replicating his performance at High-A in a more challenging environment at Double-A Bowie. Pop, like Maddux and Tewksbury before him, isn't necessarily trying to rack up strikeouts; rather, he wants to use his sinker-slider combo to induce weak contact, break bats, and get batters to put the ball on the ground, though we'll let you find what's different in the stat line between Pop and those other guys. Pop's nasty mid-90s sinker comes out of a tricky, almost sidearm, slot, and the crossfire action makes the pitch especially tough on righties. His slider also comes in at above-average speed, but could use more sharpness to be a truly plus pitch. Kentucky turns out polished major league prospects, and that's no different in the case of 2017 draftee Pop, who has sailed through the lower minors and seems poised to be contributing to a big-league bullpen soon, so everyone warm up your Magnitude from *Community* impressions.

YEAR	TEAM	LVL	AGE	WHIP	ERA	DRA	WARP	MPH	FB%	WHF	CSP
2018	GRL	A	21	1.16	2.20	2.40	0.5				
2018	RCU	A+	21	0.70	0.33	4.38	0.2				
2018	BOW	AA	21	0.94	2.53	4.07	0.2				
2019	BAL	MLB	22	1.60	5.29	5.21	-0.1				

Grayson Rodriguez   RHP

Born: 11/16/99   Age: 19   Bats: L   Throws: R
Height: 6'5"   Weight: 220   Origin: Round 1, 2018 Draft (#11 overall)

YEAR	TEAM	LVL	AGE	W	L	SV	G	GS	IP	H	HR	BB/9	K/9	K	GB%	BABIP
2018	ORI	RK	18	0	2	0	9	8	19^1	17	0	3.3	9.3	20	43%	.321
2019	BAL	MLB	19	1	3	0	11	8	31	36	6	6.2	7.1	24	42%	.314

Comparables: Jaime Barria, Bryse Wilson, Raul Alcantara

Edgar Allan Poe's "imp of the perverse" is the little devil that sits on our shoulders, willing us to do the one thing we know we should not do: sticking out a foot to trip someone down the stairs, punching a fist into the birthday cake, being the Orioles and selecting a high school arm with a first-round draft choice. Rodriguez, at least, looks big and durable: at 6'5" and 220, he dwarfed his high school contemporaries, even in Texas. The bigger question is whether he'll be able to create a sharp distinction between his curve and slider, previously thrown as one pitch. Rodriguez jumped up draft boards late in the season thanks to an ability to adjust, including improved conditioning that sent his fastball up to 96-98 at max effort, so there's an intriguing mix of tools here, and plenty of time for the Orioles to develop them, provided the imp of the perverse minds its own business.

YEAR	TEAM	LVL	AGE	WHIP	ERA	DRA	WARP	MPH	FB%	WHF	CSP
2018	ORI	RK	18	1.24	1.40	2.91	0.7				
2019	BAL	MLB	19	1.85	6.51	6.46	-0.4				

Dillon Tate RHP

Born: 05/01/94 Age: 25 Bats: R Throws: R
Height: 6'2" Weight: 195 Origin: Round 1, 2015 Draft (#4 overall)

YEAR	TEAM	LVL	AGE	W	L	SV	G	GS	IP	H	HR	BB/9	K/9	K	GB%	BABIP
2016	HIC	A	22	3	3	0	17	16	65	78	5	3.7	7.6	55	44%	.376
2016	CSC	A	22	1	0	0	7	0	17^1	21	1	3.1	7.8	15	57%	.351
2017	TAM	A+	23	6	0	0	9	9	58^1	48	4	2.3	7.1	46	61%	.262
2017	TRN	AA	23	1	2	0	4	4	25	23	3	3.2	6.1	17	56%	.270
2018	TRN	AA	24	5	2	0	15	15	82^2	67	7	2.7	8.2	75	48%	.263
2018	BOW	AA	24	2	3	0	7	7	40^2	48	3	2.0	4.6	21	63%	.324
2019	BAL	MLB	25	1	2	0	14	3	26	29	4	3.6	6.2	19	48%	.294

Breakout: 10%   Improve: 15%   Collapse: 13%   Attrition: 23%   MLB: 33%
Comparables: Alex Wilson, Sam Howard, Myles Jaye

Trades can be a blow to the player's ego; Beyonce does not write songs about being replaceable. For Tate, however, the two times he's been traded might have put him on the best path for baseball success. First, he was acquired by the Yankees as Texas, unimpressed with the former first-round pick's numbers at Single-A, shipped him off in the Carlos Beltran trade. Without directly dragging his old organization, Tate has spoken about the amount of learning he did with the Yankees in understanding his delivery and the craft of pitching. In a second exposure to Double-A, Tate's peripherals improved across the board, even as his mid-3s ERA didn't budge. Now Tate gets a shot to enact what he's learned in a significantly lower-pressure environment a few hours down the road on I-95. One red flag: Tate, who has battled injuries in his career, was shut down with shoulder soreness in late September, a similar injury to the one that derailed his first season of pro ball.

YEAR	TEAM	LVL	AGE	WHIP	ERA	DRA	WARP	MPH	FB%	WHF	CSP
2016	HIC	A	22	1.62	5.12	3.36	1.2				
2016	CSC	A	22	1.56	3.12	4.77	0.0				
2017	TAM	A+	23	1.08	2.62	3.97	0.9				
2017	TRN	AA	23	1.28	3.24	5.19	0.0				
2018	TRN	AA	24	1.11	3.38	3.18	2.1				
2018	BOW	AA	24	1.40	5.75	4.28	0.5				
2019	BAL	MLB	25	1.47	5.24	5.09	0.1				

LINEOUTS

Hitters

HITTER	POS	TEAM	LVL	AGE	PA	R	2B	3B	HR	RBI	BB	K	SB	CS	AVG/OBP/SLG	DRC+	WARP
Hanser Alberto	INF	ROU	AAA	25	384	45	17	3	7	58	9	28	0	3	.330/.346/.452	112	1.5
	INF	TEX	MLB	25	30	0	2	0	0	0	2	4	0	1	.185/.241/.259	88	0.0
Chris Bostick	CF	IND	AAA	25	327	32	24	3	4	32	24	66	6	3	.295/.351/.436	123	0.4
	CF	PIT	MLB	25	2	0	0	0	0	0	0	1	0	0	.000/.000/.000	68	0.0
	CF	NWO	AAA	25	71	6	1	0	0	6	5	19	1	1	.281/.338/.297	90	0.0
	CF	MIA	MLB	25	16	0	1	0	0	2	2	6	0	0	.214/.313/.286	69	-0.1
Jean Carmona	SS	HEL	Rk	18	172	28	8	3	4	24	13	45	5	3	.239/.298/.406	59	-0.8
	SS	ABE	A-	18	100	9	7	0	0	7	6	25	0	1	.226/.280/.301	77	-0.7
Brett Cumberland	C	BRV	A+	23	341	40	15	0	11	39	52	85	0	1	.236/.367/.407	135	1.5
	C	BOW	AA	23	49	6	0	0	3	7	4	12	0	0	.190/.292/.405	78	0.0
Adam Hall	SS	ABE	A-	19	256	35	9	3	1	24	17	58	22	5	.293/.368/.374	134	1.0
Drew Jackson	2B	TUL	AA	24	410	57	20	1	15	46	45	93	22	7	.251/.356/.447	113	1.9
Richie Martin	SS	MID	AA	23	509	68	29	8	6	42	44	86	25	10	.300/.368/.439	120	3.0
Carlos Perez	C	ATL	MLB	27	22	0	0	0	0	0	1	6	0	0	.143/.182/.143	62	-0.1
	C	ROU	AAA	27	87	10	2	0	4	13	7	12	0	0	.316/.368/.494	118	0.3
	C	TEX	MLB	27	53	1	2	0	1	3	1	15	1	0	.143/.176/.245	66	-0.2
Jace Peterson	2B	NYA	MLB	28	11	0	0	0	0	0	1	3	0	1	.300/.364/.300	73	-0.1
	2B	BAL	MLB	28	235	21	13	2	3	28	30	55	13	2	.195/.308/.325	77	0.2
Jack Reinheimer	INF	RNO	AAA	25	219	26	9	2	3	21	20	45	6	4	.237/.312/.353	79	-0.5
	INF	LVG	AAA	25	60	13	3	0	2	5	4	10	7	0	.327/.383/.491	83	0.2
	INF	NYN	MLB	25	35	4	0	0	0	0	5	9	1	1	.167/.286/.167	79	0.1
Joey Rickard	CF	NOR	AAA	27	185	25	13	1	2	27	26	28	3	0	.275/.384/.412	134	1.4
	CF	BAL	MLB	27	230	27	10	1	8	23	15	55	4	2	.244/.300/.413	92	0.6
Anthony Santander	RF	BAL	MLB	23	108	8	5	1	1	6	6	21	1	0	.198/.250/.297	75	0.0
	RF	BOW	AA	23	222	26	9	3	5	22	10	32	4	1	.258/.293/.402	87	-0.7
	RF	NOR	AAA	23	47	3	3	0	2	7	2	9	0	0	.182/.213/.386	80	0.0
Dwight Smith	LF	BUF	AAA	25	361	39	25	1	6	42	44	53	9	3	.268/.358/.413	128	1.5
	LF	TOR	MLB	25	75	9	8	0	2	8	7	13	0	0	.262/.347/.477	99	0.1
Jesus Sucre	C	TBA	MLB	30	198	9	5	0	1	17	9	29	1	0	.209/.247/.253	73	-0.3
Andrew Susac	C	BAL	MLB	28	26	1	1	0	0	0	12	0	0	.115/.115/.154	57	-0.1
	C	NOR	AAA	28	158	15	7	0	6	26	31	42	0	0	.256/.405/.456	145	1.6
Eric Young	LF	SLC	AAA	33	348	46	18	7	5	34	35	66	10	6	.300/.367/.453	102	-0.5
	LF	ANA	MLB	33	117	12	4	2	1	8	6	28	5	1	.202/.248/.303	59	-0.1

Hanser Alberto got back to the big leagues with the Rangers after battling a shoulder injury and then got claimed off waivers by the Yankees. His nickname is "Radio" because of a habit of calling play-by-play for games while playing in them. ⓘ Already traded three times before turning 23, **Chris Bostick**'s redeeming quality is his ability to play nearly every position. But without an outstanding glove, and with a forgettable, light bat, he's on his way to

Baltimore Orioles 2019

journeyman status. ⓧ **Jean Carmona** is a low-level lottery ticket obtained from Milwaukee in the Scoop deal, an infielder with a plus arm who can help prop up a system that's gone less for Harlem Globetrotters and more for Harlem Meatpackers. Good bat speed and some natural loft to his swing suggest Carmona might have more power to show as the 18-year-old adds strength. ⓧ The Orioles are perilously low on catching prospects, so acquiring bat-first **Brett Cumberland** from the Braves in the Gausman deal wasn't a bad idea. His new team made the curious decision to send him to the instructional league rather than the AFL, where he'd face tougher competition and get reps with higher-level pitching, indicating they aren't as worried about his bat as the need to develop his receiving skills. ⓧ There is a Stanford computer scientist named **Craig Gentry** who specializes in cryptology and writes papers with inscrutable and yet saucy titles like "Noncommutative Determinant is Hard: A Simple Proof Using an Extension of Barrington's Theorem" and "The Geometry of Provable Security: Some Proofs of Security in Which Lattices Make a Surprise Appearance." Baseball's Craig Gentry, released by the Orioles in September, could do with borrowing some of this insouciant swag, the mark of someone who has such mastery over a subject as to be able to play with it. ⓧ Born in Bermuda, **Adam Hall** convinced his parents to let him move to Canada as a preteen so he could have a shot at a baseball career. A legitimate shortstop, Hall started off slow this season at short-season Aberdeen but finished strong, winning Minor League Player of the Month honors after a torrid August where he slashed .390/.462/.524. ⓧ **Drew Jackson** is a plus defender at either second base or shortstop and even showed that he could hit for some power outside of the California League for the first time. He could be one of the first names called on if the Dodgers need some middle infield reinforcements in 2019. ⓧ **Richie Martin** began hitting the ball with authority at Double-A in 2018, which is what you hope eventually happens when you draft a top defensive shortstop and throw him to the professional-pitching wolves. You don't have to hit *that* much if you've got Martin's defensive profile, so there's now a light at the end of his development tunnel. ⓧ **Carlos Perez** is a Jeff Mathis type: defense first, hit later. The Rangers opted to instead sign the real Jeff Mathis. ⓧ Another inhabitant of Lord Baltimore's Home for Wayward Former Prospects, the Orioles picked **Jace Peterson** up off waivers from the Yankees to serve as the standard Gritty Veteran Utilityman for 2018. Peterson still possesses the excellent plate discipline he's shown throughout his minors career, but he's no more than a warm body in the O's infield. ⓧ After years of a Woodrow Wilson-esque isolationist approach to the international market, the Orioles decided to dip a toe in the birdbath and started hoarding international slot money towards the end of the 2018 season. Their first two signings were 16-year-old shortstop **Moises Ramirez** and 19-year-old RHP Carlos Del Rosario, both out of the Dominican Republic. Look for the O's to be much more active internationally now that the Angelos scions have more control of the club's activities. ⓧ Utility infielder **Jack Reinheimer** leveraged another bad offensive season into a cup of coffee in the majors, and while he did record his first major-league hit this time, he's not likely to be any team's first, second or third choice at shortstop. ⓧ **Joey Rickard** collecting almost 800 plate appearances for the Orioles over the last three seasons is irrefutable proof the Mandela Effect is real, even if it targets mostly light-hitting outfielders. ⓧ **Anthony Santander** made Baltimore's 25-man after a strong spring but failed to translate that to in-season production. He was optioned back to Double-A in mid-May and was not recalled from Triple-A when rosters expanded. ⓧ If second-generation ballplayers were a Westerosi army, **Dwight Smith** would be leading the vanguard in the march on Toronto. Though often being the first to arrive also means being the first to be discarded when the real battle comes. ⓧ **Jesus Sucre** was among MLB's worst hitters last season and, despite a reputation from teammates as a plus behind the plate, the numbers there also frowned upon him. ⓧ Former catching prospect **Andrew Susac** now has more trades (two) than healthy seasons (one) under his belt since 2016. He still might be Baltimore's best backstop? ⓧ **Eric Young, Jr.** has a career 80 percent stolen base success rate, 50th best in the history of baseball. Since this is a family reference book, we will not mention any of the other numbers.

Baltimore Orioles 2019

Pitchers

PITCHER	TEAM	LVL	AGE	W	L	SV	G	GS	IP	H	HR	BB/9	K/9	K	GB%	WHIP	ERA	DRA	WARP
Pedro Araujo	BAL	MLB	24	1	3	0	20	0	28	29	9	5.8	9.3	29	36%	1.68	7.71	4.07	0.3
Michael Baumann	DEL	A	22	5	0	0	7	7	38	23	0	3.1	11.1	47	53%	0.95	1.42	3.25	0.9
	FRD	A+	22	8	5	0	17	17	92^2	82	9	3.9	5.7	59	35%	1.32	3.88	8.09	-3.0
Tyler Erwin	FRD	A+	23	4	4	18	50	0	68^1	45	1	3.0	11.1	84	53%	1.00	1.58	2.93	1.6
Gray Fenter	DEL	A	22	3	3	0	14	2	26^2	31	2	4.4	10.5	31	38%	1.65	6.75	4.39	0.2
	ABE	A-	22	5	3	0	13	11	57	41	5	3.9	9.5	60	39%	1.16	3.95	3.63	1.0
Paul Fry	BOW	AA	25	3	0	2	15	0	19	10	2	5.2	13.3	28	68%	1.11	2.84	2.70	0.5
	NOR	AAA	25	0	1	0	13	1	23^1	22	2	1.5	11.2	29	53%	1.11	3.47	2.52	0.7
	BAL	MLB	25	1	2	2	35	0	37^2	33	1	3.6	8.6	36	58%	1.27	3.35	4.17	0.3
Sean Gilmartin	MEM	AAA	28	4	2	0	24	6	46^1	48	6	3.1	6.4	33	36%	1.38	4.66	3.40	1.0
	NOR	AAA	28	2	0	0	7	3	14^1	13	1	1.3	7.5	12	37%	1.05	3.14	4.21	0.2
	BAL	MLB	28	1	1	0	12	0	27	23	4	3.7	5.0	15	46%	1.26	3.00	6.15	-0.4
Branden Kline	FRD	A+	26	1	0	2	12	0	20^2	20	0	1.3	10.0	23	36%	1.11	1.31	3.27	0.4
	BOW	AA	26	4	4	15	32	0	45	32	3	3.0	9.6	48	45%	1.04	1.80	3.11	1.0
Evan Phillips	ATL	MLB	23	0	0	0	4	0	6^1	6	3	5.7	4.3	3	41%	1.58	8.53	5.71	-0.1
	GWN	AAA	23	4	4	8	31	0	40^2	28	1	3.1	13.1	59	51%	1.03	1.99	2.52	1.2
	NOR	AAA	23	0	2	0	8	0	10^2	6	1	2.5	11.0	13	32%	0.84	3.38	3.39	0.2
	BAL	MLB	23	0	1	0	5	1	5^1	7	2	10.1	8.4	5	39%	2.44	18.56	9.68	-0.3
Josh Rogers	SWB	AAA	23	6	8	0	19	19	109^1	118	13	2.4	6.8	83	42%	1.34	3.95	4.48	1.3
	NOR	AAA	23	2	1	0	5	5	30^1	26	3	2.1	5.3	18	41%	1.09	2.08	4.60	0.3
	BAL	MLB	23	1	2	0	3	3	11^2	17	2	3.9	4.6	6	40%	1.89	8.49	7.73	-0.3
Bo Schultz	BRD	A+	32	0	0	0	8	0	10^2	2	0	3.4	8.4	10	65%	0.56	0.00	3.77	0.1
	IND	AAA	32	0	1	3	24	0	27	29	0	3.3	7.3	22	54%	1.44	2.00	3.67	0.5
Alex Wells	FRD	A+	21	7	8	0	24	24	135	142	19	2.2	6.7	101	36%	1.30	3.47	4.49	1.3
Gabriel Ynoa	BOW	AA	25	0	0	0	2	2	7	6	1	0.0	7.7	6	45%	0.86	2.57	5.18	0.0

Dan Duquette Customary Rule 5 Pick **Pedro Araujo** went down with an elbow injury in early June and was never seen again. Rule 5 picks: a reminder that generally, you get what you pay for. ⓥ **Michael Baumann** was drafted in 2017 out of Jacksonville University, which is a real school and not the faux alma mater of Jason from *The Good Place*. Even though the school's Wikipedia page counts among its notable alumni Leonard Skinner, namesake of the band Lynyrd Skynyrd; but somehow this is a real school, really. ⓥ **Tyler Erwin** is the great-great-great nephew of James K. Polk, a maniacally productive president who achieved all his major, sweeping goals in office in just one term. While it's unclear if Erwin will be as productive as his famous forbear, the 23rd-round pick was one of the best relievers in the Carolina League this season despite a fastball that averages in the high 80s thanks to excellent command, a funky three-quarters delivery, and a bulldog mentality on the mound. ⓥ Prep arm **Gray Fenter**, drafted and paid overslot in the seventh round in 2015, is now over a year removed from TJ surgery and able to mix in his curve and changeup with abandon. His low-90s fastball plays up in limited outings and might point to a future bullpen role, especially if the command doesn't sort itself out. ⚾ **Paul Fry** stepped in as the designated lefty after Richard Bleier went down with injury and was quietly effective whenever the Orioles happened to wander into a high-leverage situation. He still allows too many walks for a lefty who sits low-90s with his fastball, but the funky, sharp-breaking slider is an effective putaway pitch. ⚾ One way to explain **Sean Gilmartin's** itinerant career path is that he has a punch card where if he plays for eight different teams, he can turn it in for a long-term contract. The other is he's barely good enough to be on a major league roster. ⚾ **Branden Kline** is a 2012 draftee who's had trouble staying on the mound, missing a large chunk of 2013 with a broken ankle, and most of 2015-2017 with Tommy John. Now a reliever with a mid to upper-90s fastball, Kline has been working as a closer, converting 17-of-18 save opportunities this season, and looks on track to finally make it to Baltimore some time next season. ⚾ An under-the-radar pickup from Atlanta in the Gausman trade, **Evan Phillips** has a lively arm but has struggled with command issues. "One adjustment away" is the pitcher equivalent of "triple shy of the cycle," but if Phillips can figure out how to curtail his walks, the O's have a strong middle to back-end relief option. ⚾ It's never a good sign for anyone involved when a pitcher gets shut down twice in the same year, but that's where the Orioles wound up with **Josh Rogers**, fourth piece in the Britton trade. They actually sent him home in mid-September just to keep it from happening again. ⚾ An aspiring journalist in college way back in 2004, **Bo Schultz** says he might go back to journalism when his career is over. He might have to put that dream on hold, since he was good enough to be organizational depth for the Pirates until forearm soreness shut him down in July. ⚾ Bespectacled Australian brothers **Alex** and Lachlan **Wells** are both in organized baseball; Lachlan, who has a couple more ticks on his fastball, signed with the Twins a year earlier than Alex signed with the Orioles. What Alex lacks in velocity he makes up for with 60-grade command and a plus changeup. ⚾ Acquired for cash from the Mets, the Orioles failed to read the part of the medical report that disclosed Fred Wilpon holding **Gabriel Ynoa** by the shin when dipping him in the East River. After a relatively productive 2017 for the O's, Ynoa pitched only seven innings at Double-A this year before being shut down with recurring shin splints, and a shoulder injury to boot.

Orioles Prospects

The State of the System:
The rebuild has begun. It's, uh, gonna take a while.

The Top Ten:

1. Yusniel Diaz OF   OFP: 60   Likely: 55   ETA: Late 2019
Born: 10/07/96   Age: 22   Bats: R   Throws: R   Height: 6'1"   Weight: 195
Origin: International Free Agent, 2015

The Report: Diaz's bat carried him to the top of this list. He has excellent hand-eye coordination and solid quick-twitch which allows him to barrel the ball even though his swing can lengthen at times. The longer swing allows him to tap into his average raw power, although his swing plane is a bit flat and his hardest contact comes on low line drives. He has a patient approach with an excellent feel for the zone and quality pitch recognition. He could be a fine hitter without any further adjustments, but the flat plane seems exactly the type of swing that the Dodgers would have tweaked to unlock more XBH power. Now he's with the Orioles in a transitory time; it will be interesting to see if the player development staff has any adjustments in mind.

Diaz is an average runner and, as he's completely filled out, he will likely remain one for a while. He has solid instincts in the outfield and an above-average arm, which should allow him to be fringy in center or above average in right. Diaz can be too aggressive on the basepaths and he probably won't be much of a base-stealing threat.

Even with a solid defensive profile in right, Diaz will need to hit to provide significant value. Fortunately for O's fans, he's a good bet to do so. His fluid athleticism and hand-eye coordination should fuel above-average production with room for more if a swing adjustment unlocks more pop.

The Risks: Low. Diaz is about ready for prime time, although there's a small chance that big-league pitchers will exploit his lengthy swing enough to limit him to platoon duty. His power needs to play at least fringe-average for him to be an above-average regular, and there's a chance that that adjustment never happens.

Ben Carsley's Fantasy Take: Diaz is a good fantasy prospect, but his valuation should fluctuate pretty heavily based on your league size. Do you play in The Dynasty Guru Experts (TDGX) League-sized formats with 20-plus teams? If so, Diaz is an easy top-50 dynasty prospect as someone who's a safe bet to become an everyday regular. In shallower formats, Diaz may end up as more of just A Guy, albeit one who contributes solidly across the board. From a fantasy perspective, we've compared his ceiling to prime Melky Cabrera in the past, and that still feels apt. He's got a very clear path to playing time to boot.

2. Ryan Mountcastle 3B
OFP: 60   Likely: 50   ETA: 2020
Born: 02/18/97   Age: 22   Bats: R   Throws: R   Height: 6'3"   Weight: 195
Origin: Round 1, 2015 Draft (#36 overall)

The Report: A scouting cliché we reference often on the prospect team: "When in doubt, just pick the best hitter." His power may or may not come. He may or may not stick up the middle. But if he hits, who cares, really? Ryan Mountcastle can hit. His swing gets long from time-to-time, usually when he's trying to add leverage to get his plus raw power into play, but when everything is working it just looks right. We do think the power will come, and if he's a 60 hit/55 power bat, so what about the rest, really?

I suppose we do have to cover it though. So, the rest: Mountcastle has a well-below-average arm, so third base is unlikely to work out any better than shortstop did, despite adequate instincts and hands for the hot corner. It's possible Mountcastle could handle second, but he could grow off the keystone as well, making left field or even first base a more likely long-term defensive home. That puts significant pressure on the bat to play to projection.

The Risks: Medium. We love the bat, and he conquered Double-A at 21, but it's unclear where Mountcastle will end up on the defensive spectrum.

Ben Carsley's Fantasy Take: For my money, Mountcastle is the best fantasy prospect in the system and one of my favorite pure bats in all the minors. There are some warts, sure, but it's also easy to see Mountcastle following the Nick Castellanos career path and blooming into a top-10 fantasy third baseman or top-25 fantasy outfielder. Count any years you get 3B/CI eligibility out of him as a blessing, and bank on a .280-plus average with 20 bombs and solid R/RBI totals for the long haul.

3. DL Hall LHP
OFP: 60   Likely: 50   ETA: Late 2020
Born: 09/19/98   Age: 20   Bats: L   Throws: L   Height: 6'2"   Weight: 195
Origin: Round 1, 2017 Draft (#21 overall)

The Report: Baltimore's 2017 first-round pick had a strong full-season debut and spent the entire year as a 19-year-old in the South Atlantic League. Beyond the eye-popping top line stats, Hall looks every bit the part of a high-ranking lefty prospect arm. His fastball sits in the mid-90s and can touch higher. It's a heavy pitch which he will also cut, and it shows late life when he wants to elevate it for a strikeout. He pairs it with a power curve that flashes plus. It's a big, tight breaker that he can start in the zone and entice chases, or drop in for a strike.

Hall's slider and change lag behind at present. The slider is shorter and shows a different look with average depth at times, but is too often a flat 10-4 offering. The straight change benefits from his deceptive arm action, but is well below average at present, and hangs in the zone too often.

Mechanically, Hall has some things to iron out as well. It's an uptempo but inconsistent delivery that leaves his upper and lower halves out of sync at times. He'll throw across his body with slingy arm action and a bit of crossfire. That adds deception to the fastball, but also makes the command projection more average than plus. He won't always finish his pitches off and will miss armside and up here and there. If you guessed that Hall is a mid-rotation starting pitching prospect who needs to improve his command and third pitch, congratulations, you've been here before. Did you remember your punch card? There will be plenty more arms like this to come over the next couple hundred of pages as well.

The Risks: High. I believe we used the "He's an Orioles pitching prospect named "DL" joke a fair bit last year. So this year I will just point out that a pre-draft comp I got from a prospect team member was Scott Kazmir. So yeah, those risks…

Ben Carsley's Fantasy Take:

The thing about Hall is that he's an Orioles pitching prospect. Maybe the front office overhaul in Baltimore will lead to better results for this particular breed of dynasty asset, but I'll believe it when I see it. There's enough upside and a short enough timeline here that you can make Hall a top-200 guy if you want to. I won't, because I'm a cynic.

4 **Grayson Rodriguez   RHP**   OFP: 60   Likely: 45   ETA: 2023
Born: 11/16/99   Age: 19   Bats: L   Throws: R   Height: 6'5"   Weight: 220
Origin: Round 1, 2018 Draft (#11 overall)

The Report: Rodriguez ticks almost every box on the "first-round-Texas-prep-arm" checklist. He lags behind the standard a bit in projectability, but that's only because he's already a very large human. He has the requisite big fastball, sitting around 95 and touching the upper-90s at times. He has a potential plus secondary in the arsenal as well, a power slider with good late tilt.

The rest of the four-pitch mix is below-average—which, granted, is also one of the boxes here. Rodriguez works in a loopy curve and a developing change to round out his repertoire. The mechanics don't scream "slam-dunk-starter" either, as he is very upright and stiff, without much leg drive, and he relies on his arm speed and late torque to hit 98. The arm action is inconsistent and high-effort as well. Still, there are worse building blocks for a pitching prospect than a well-developed 6-foot-5 frame and a potential plus fastball/slider combo.

The Risks: High. He's a prep arm in the complex who needs to develop his secondaries and he has relatively high reliever risk.

Ben Carsley's Fantasy Take: Too long a lead time, too low of a fantasy ceiling and too much an Oriole. Check back next year.

5. Ryan McKenna OF

OFP: 55 Likely: 45 ETA: Early 2020
Born: 02/14/97 Age: 22 Bats: R Throws: R Height: 5'11" Weight: 185
Origin: Round 4, 2015 Draft (#133 overall)

The Report: A major-league average (50) tool grade doesn't get much effusive praise around these parts. There are some selection bias issues here. The players who make these lists generally have a standout tool or two to fill out the 200-word count for our blurbs. McKenna offers no such easy narrative. He does everything averagely well. That is major-league average though. And it's easy to forget how impressive average major-league talent is. His hit tool—yes, it's a five—presents as short to the ball with above-average barrel control. It's more of a line drive swing, but there's enough leverage that he will get to most of his 50 raw power in play. He's an average center fielder with an average arm. While he's a plus runner at present, he figures to slow down into the average to solid-average range in the majors. It's not quite the five-tool center fielder we tend to rave about—the game power will likely play below-average with some pull-side pop against lefties—but McKenna has turned himself into a quality major-league prospect. It's coincidental that he slots in at #5 in the system, but it does create a nice bit of rankinative determinism.

The Risks: Medium. McKenna hasn't aced Double-A yet and may lack a carrying a tool. Sometimes the average-across-the-board guys play up, other times we find out they aren't actually average-across-the-board. If you want to look for positive risk, he is a cold weather prep bat who just had a bit of a breakout season, which can be a positive marker for additional growth.

Ben Carsley's Fantasy Take: Given the balanced overall skill set, his proximity to the majors and the fact that he could play in a very favorable home park, it's safe to say McKenna is a better fantasy prospect than an IRL one. The risk is that his tweener profile pushes him out of everyday playing time, but given the dearth of talent on the O's roster at present, hopefully he can stave off such a future. McKenna doesn't profile as a guy who'll win you any leagues, but could he be well-rounded enough to push his way to OF4 or OF5 status in deeper formats? Sure. He probably won't make the top-101, but he might make a top-150.

6. Dillon Tate RHP

OFP: 55 Likely: 45 ETA: 2019
Born: 05/01/94 Age: 25 Bats: R Throws: R Height: 6'2" Weight: 195
Origin: Round 1, 2015 Draft (#4 overall)

The Report: Put aside his draft status as the fourth overall pick three-and-a-half years ago and what you have is a 95-and-a-slider guy with terribly inconsistent performance due to command that comes and goes. The fastball is pretty straight. He doesn't always hold his velocity well. It's a plus-flashing slider, but one of the things that's changed in baseball over the last decade is that a whole lot of pitchers have a plus-flashing slider now. The changeup still isn't quite what you want. The fastball/slider combo can be good enough, and the changeup isn't hopeless. Even coming off a hideous end to the season as a 24-year-old in Double-A, there's still flickering hope for a mid-rotation arm. He's also pitched better at times out of the pen, and the stigma on dumping your top pitching prospects there is dissipating. At some point though, someone's developmental clock ticks long enough that you stop giving him the benefit of the doubt; the guys selected two picks ahead of Tate and three picks behind him were also college draftees of the same age, and both are already established MLB stars.

The Risks: Well, there's a heck of a lot of signs here he's going to end up in the bullpen, aren't there? Strictly speaking we aren't supposed to care about the organizational change when writing him up, but the Orioles pitching development has become an industry punchline, and he was much worse after the trade. There's also a long history of underperformance here, such that he's gotten traded twice now already.

Ben Carsley's Fantasy Take: Well, if you've held on to Tate all this time, I guess you can take the fact that he's somewhat dynasty-relevant again as a good sign. But the real question is: why did you hold on to Tate this long? He's bounced around multiple organizations that would be terrible for his future fantasy value, and the odds that he's just a frustrating reliever in the end are too high. You gotta know when to hold em, know when to fold em, know when to walk away, etc.

7 **Keegan Akin   LHP**   OFP: 50   Likely: 45   ETA: Late 2019
Born: 04/01/95   Age: 24   Bats: L   Throws: L   Height: 6'0"   Weight: 225
Origin: Round 2, 2016 Draft (#54 overall)

The Report: Last year Akin slotted in at seventh in a below-average Orioles system as your typical funky lefty starter with a decent change-up and a fastball around 90. This year he slots in at seven once again, but both he and the system are markedly improved. It's easy to peg the culprit here. Akin's fastball has jumped to 93-95 and touches 97. The plus velo—combined with a hitchy, deceptive delivery, a bit of gloveside run, and above-average command—generated a lot of late swings from Double-A hitters. While Akin never had a frame you would call "projectable," the velocity bump makes his fastball a borderline plus-plus offering at its best. The fastball will need to carry the profile here as the changeup is merely average and the slider below that. The latter is a flat 1-8 offering that breaks enough to keep it off barrels most of the time, but lacks the depth to consistently miss bats. The improved fastball hasn't markedly changed the ceiling here, but it makes Akin more likely to have a substantial major-league career.

The Risks: Low. As a close-to-the-majors lefty with now plus velocity and a bit of funk, Akin is a low-ceiling guy, but likely to get major-league opportunities.

Ben Carsley's Fantasy Take: If you read the DL Hall blurb and thought "I just wish this prospect had less upside," Akin is the guy for you. Also why is every Orioles lefty's name a synonym for being in pain?

8   **Austin Hays   OF**   OFP: 50   Likely: 45   ETA: Debuted in 2017
Born: 07/05/95   Age: 23   Bats: R   Throws: R   Height: 6'1"   Weight: 195
Origin: Round 3, 2016 Draft (#91 overall)

The Report: This feels unfair to Hays who broke out across two levels in 2017 and made the majors that September. While we weren't quite as high on his ultimate ceiling as some of our prospect-ranking counterparts, we did have him comfortably as a Top 101 guy, and the second best prospect in the system. How'd he do in 2018? Well, he was bad and then he was hurt. This ranking may be a bit of an overreaction, but let's zoom out a bit.

Hays had about a half-season of Double-A baseball before his call-up. Now he has about a season and has posted a slugging-heavy .829 OPS at appropriate prospect ages. He had to have offseason ankle surgery to remedy the issue that limited him to a half-season last year. There are mitigating factors all over his 2018, and honestly the ordinal distance between him and Ryan McKenna overstates the gap as prospects. That said, like McKenna he is a "sum of the average tools" guy and doesn't even have McKenna's glove in center. When you get evidence that one of those 50-55 offensive tools might not play to projection, the whole profile becomes far riskier.

The Risks: Low. While we aren't quite as sold on the plus regular ceiling as we were last year, a healthy Hays should be a productive major-league piece in 2019.

Ben Carsley's Fantasy Take: Hays was a guy I liked a lot a year ago, and I'm not ready to jump ship just yet. He's got a clear path to playing time (stop me if you've heard that before) and while he's not the defender McKenna is, his fantasy profile is starkly similar. He might just be a fourth outfielder, sure, but fourth outfielders who play every day because their teams are bad can still have some value.

9   **Luis Ortiz   RHP**   OFP: 50   Likely: 40   ETA: Debuted in 2018
Born: 09/22/95   Age: 23   Bats: R   Throws: R   Height: 6'3"   Weight: 230
Origin: Round 1, 2014 Draft (#30 overall)

The Report: It feels like we have been writing about Ortiz forever. You know the cliff notes by now—hefty righty, plus fastball, oft-injured, traded twice. Well, the fastball isn't quite plus anymore, whether due to his litany of maladies or just normal pitching prospect attrition. His fastball sits more in the low-90s now, touching 95. It still features good run and sink when it's down in the zone, but it's very hittable when elevated, and his velocity can tick down into the upper-80s later in starts. The movement keeps the pitch above-average and covers at times for average command. Ortiz fills out his repertoire with an average change that works off the fastball well with similar movement in the low-80s; an average, mid-80s slider with short, late tilt; and a fringy curve he steals strikes with now and again. He's no longer a Top 101 candidate, and he still has durability issues: He missed a month early in the year and left his first big-league start with a pulled hamstring. But he's reached the majors and is now with an organization that will have, uh, let's say "starting pitching opportunities" in the short-to-medium term.

The Risks: Medium. Ortiz got a cup of coffee in the majors, but he didn't exactly look great, and has still never thrown 100 innings in a season.

Ben Carsley's Fantasy Take: Well, if innings pitched is your league's only pitching category, Ortiz might end up being decent. If you care about scary things like ERA, WHIP and W, however, Ortiz is best left to the waiver wire.

10 Jean Carlos Encarnacion 3B

OFP: 50   Likely: 45   ETA: 2021
Born: 01/17/98   Age: 21   Bats: R   Throws: R   Height: 6'3"   Weight: 195
Origin: International Free Agent, 2016

The Report: Encarnacion was one of the most polarizing reports in the South Atlantic League. Reports varied considerably depending on when the evaluator saw him. The easy tools to nail down are his raw power, which will end up at least plus, and an above-average arm that plays at third. He has the swing to tap into this power, with big lift and extension out front. How much he gets to in games is the question.

Encarnacion is susceptible to basic sequencing, and his lengthy cut suggests that there will likely be plenty of swing and miss long-term. His swing will look different from one at-bat to the next, and between that and his lack of discipline, he projects as a below-average hitter. Encarnacion's glove is equally iffy. He has smooth actions at times, but he'll take plays off and goes to the backhand too often. He needs to make strides to stick at third, but he has the athleticism to stick there as a fringe-average defender. Ultimately, Encarnacion's tools suggest a high-ceiling corner-infield slugger with huge projection, but the gap between his present and potential abilities is massive, and will require time and patience.

The Risks: Very High. The gap between Encarnacion's present and potential is huge. A lackadaisical approach at times doesn't help, but athletic actions and size are in his favor.

Ben Carsley's Fantasy Take: Encarnacion is a good one for your watch list, but the risk/reward mix isn't favorable enough to make him a truly meaningfully dynasty asset yet. Keep an eye on him though, and pick him up in deeper leagues if the power plays at High-A.

The Next Five:

11 Bruce Zimmermann   LHP
Born: 02/09/95   Age: 24   Bats: L   Throws: L   Height: 6'2"   Weight: 215
Origin: Round 5, 2017 Draft (#140 overall)

Zimmermann is an advanced left-hander with the command to carve up the minor leagues and the stuff of an up-and-down guy or long reliever. His fringy fastball doesn't have much life or movement, but it sits in the low-90s and plays up because of his command. The better secondary varies from start to start, but his changeup has greater potential at solid-average with fade and arm speed. The breaker should settle at fringe-average with moderate bite and depth. Zimmermann is maxed out physically and he has a durable frame conducive to eating innings. Players like this tend to produce in the minors before big-league hitters expose the limitations of a pitchability arm without a dominant secondary.

12 Adam Hall   SS
Born: 05/22/99   Age: 20   Bats: R   Throws: R   Height: 6'0"   Weight: 170
Origin: Round 2, 2017 Draft (#60 overall)

A second-round pick out of a Canadian high school, Hall has good instincts at short and covers a lot of ground at the six. He's less physical than most other prospects in his draft orbit. He looks shorter than his listed height—six feet on the dot in the media guide—and he's not especially toolsy. He does make plenty of contact and he's a disciplined hitter, so he's not a total black hole at the plate. Ultimately though, Hall's more of a reliable defender with an adequate bat than any kind of building block.

13 Zac Lowther   LHP
Born: 04/30/96   Age: 23   Bats: L   Throws: L   Height: 6'2"   Weight: 235
Origin: Round 2, 2017 Draft (#74 overall)

Lowther lacks a blazing fastball, true out pitch, or elite command, but he still pitched well across two levels in 2018. The southpaw's success stems from his deceptive motion. He works from a low three-quarters arm slot, and uses a long stride to get his arm over the front of his body. Hitters don't see the ball well and that helps his pedestrian velocity play up. Lowther also has an above-average curveball with depth; his slider and changeup are both fringy. He works both sides of the plate well, and his plus command could allow him to stick as a No. 5 starter.

14 Alex Wells   LHP
Born: 02/27/97   Age: 22   Bats: L   Throws: L   Height: 6'1"   Weight: 190
Origin: International Free Agent, 2015

Alex Wells is the same sort of funky-lefty-with-a-change as Keegan Akin. If you really, really prefer fastball command to fastball velocity you could even get Wells ahead of Akin…I suppose. I won't be going there. Wells' fastball is pinned around 90, and while his command and change are probably a half-grade better than Akin's, the breaker is similarly a show-me pitch. Wells just has far less margin for error at 89-91, so he's more likely to land at the swingman end of his outcome range.

15 Cadyn Grenier   SS
Born: 10/31/96   Age: 22   Bats: R   Throws: R   Height: 5'11"   Weight: 188
Origin: Round 1, 2018 Draft (#37 overall)

Grenier got plenty of amateur scouting coverage this year as Nick Madrigal's double play partner at Oregon State, and the Orioles popped him with the 37th overall pick. While the White Sox are trying to slide Madrigal to the left side, Grenier is likely to stay at 6 for a while at least. It's not a frame you usually associate with shortstop, but Grenier is an above-average runner who moves well in the field. The arm is perhaps a bit light for the left side, and if his frame continues to mature, he might be forced to slide to second base. The offensive question marks loom larger, as the swing is a little stiff (although he'll show decent feel with the barrel head) and there's more swing-and-miss than you'd prefer in your comp-round college bat. Grenier is likely a fifth infielder, although there's a chance the profile coalesces into a second-division type if he sticks at short or the bat improves with pro reps.

Others of note:

Brett Cumberland, C, Double-A Bowie
Cumberland has enough bat to reach the major leagues in a backup or up-and-down role, but any defensive value at all would lift that projection. Right now, he's a bat-first guy with above-average power and advanced plate discipline: He'll never hit for average, but the home runs and walks will carry the profile at the plate. His defensive future is still in question, but to his credit, he's made strides behind the plate. Even so, fringy athleticism and slow feet limit his ceiling

Baltimore Orioles 2019

back there. Without a clear defensive home, he may get the dreaded Quad-A label. He fits best on an American League team, and getting dealt from Atlanta can only help his career.

D.J. Stewart, OF, Baltimore Orioles

We wrote last year that Stewart would need to keep hitting to keep his Top Ten Orioles prospect status (the lowest tier of Starwood Preferred Member). While the system improved around him, Stewart's performance with the bat was more mixed. Most of the power surge from 2017 remained, but overall Stewart didn't mash as much as you'd like in Triple-A. He did reach Baltimore in September and did hit there, but the profile remains a tough sell. He's a fringy corner outfielder and has never hit as much as you'd like to overcome the profile issues. It's hard to project more than 4 hit/5 pop here, and it doesn't help that the Orioles have other fringy corner outfielders, but Stewart is going to end up higher on the Roster Resource depth chart than you'd think.

Dean Kremer, RHP, Double-A Bowie

The Dodgers moved Kremer from relief to starting this year at Rancho. Usually scuffling college arms go in the opposite direction, but Kremer popped in longer stints despite his previous mid-90s fastball in the pen sitting in the low-90s when stretched out. The heater plays up due to Kremer's extension and slight crossfire, which makes it sneak up on hitters. He has a full four-pitch arsenal with both breaking balls ahead of the change. The curve shows good 12-6 action, and Kremer can spot it or get chases down and away. The slider has been his out pitch and he can manipulate it as well. The change is the clear fourth pitch here and the lack of an armside option against lefties might make Kremer more of a multi-inning reliever or swingman than backend starter. This isn't significantly different from most of the arms above, and you could go a lot of different ways with a pref list after the top five in this improving but still shallow Orioles system.

Zach Pop, RHP, Double-A Bowie

Pop is your prototypical, fastball/slider relief prospect. He's already on the express track to the majors, having blitzed three minor league levels in 2018 on the back of his mid-90s fastball and potential plus slider. Despite his tall and lanky frame, Pop keeps everything pretty compact and throws strikes consistently. His fastball features good tail from his low-three-quarters slot, and he's grown more comfortable manipulating the slider in his first full pro season. It's not a consistently plus pitch yet, but he'll throw a hard backfoot one to righties often enough to project it getting there, and soon. Pop could be 7th or 8th inning help for the Orioles in 2019, and given the state of the O's bullpen, he might even be up before soft-shell crab season starts.

Michael Baumann, RHP, Advanced-A Frederick

Despite a successful season across two A-ball levels, this Michael Baumann still can't top his own Google search results. Maybe he needs to tweet about Rod Sex to drive those page hits on his baseball-reference page. Now major-league b-ref pages tend to show up atop dudes writing about college baseball and Hulu originals, and this Michael Baumann certainly has a shot to earn one on the strength of his big fastball. The mid-90s heater flashes good life up, although it can run a bit true below the letters. Baumann has two fringy breakers, and the curve and slider can bleed together a bit. He has the frame to log innings, but the stuff is more middle relief. And while the high hard one missed bats in the Sally, Carolina League hitters were fooled far less. Still, if he does make the show, maybe the other Baumann will finally buy some non-Gamecock baseball gear.

Hunter Harvey, RHP, Double-A Bowie

Hunter Harvey is hurt again and didn't throw at instructs. He did pitch 32 innings in 2018, which is the most he's thrown since 2014. Harvey also got a major league call-up back in April, but didn't get into a game. Given what happened after, it might be a Moonlight Graham type of scenario, although Graham didn't have Harvey's pure stuff. There are plenty of pitchers who have put together careers where they were either "very good or unavailable." Harvey might end up one of them, but the ratio has skewed way too much towards "unavailable" thus far during his pro career.

Top Talents 25 and Under (born 4/1/93 or later):

1. Yusniel Diaz
2. Ryan Mountcastle
3. Cedric Mullins
4. DL Hall
5. Grayson Rodriguez
6. Chance Sisco
7. Ryan McKenna
8. Dillon Tate
9. Keegan Akin
10. Austin Hays

Cedric Mullins is just barely ineligible for the prospect list, having taken over duties in center late in the season. With Adam Jones gone, he seems to have a clear shot at the job. As has been the case virtually throughout the minors, he was completely hopeless batting right-handed, and we're well past the point of openly wondering why he's still switch-hitting. He profiles as a nifty platoon center fielder, which in this organization qualifies as a huge developmental success.

Chance Sisco, on the other hand, has not developed much at all lately. He's stuck at catcher, which is good, because his bat won't support a corner position at this point. Catchers often develop oddly and late, and there's absolutely a latent hit tool somewhere down there, but the dude couldn't even shove aside Caleb Joseph and Austin Wynns to claim more playing time on a team that went 47-115.

The Orioles have a half-dozen or so more guys that aren't prospect-eligible but are eligible here. They just aren't better than Austin Hays moving forward. (Trust us, we wanted to get Gabriel Ynoa in here somewhere.) It's going to be a long rebuild.

Part 3: Featured Articles

The Hole in The Shift is Fixing Itself

Russell Carleton

I've been on a bit of a mission against The Shift of late. I'm not out to get The Shift for the usual reasons that people oppose it. The words "the right way to play the game" won't be found on my lips. If a team wants to pursue a strategy that is within the rules and it works, then by all means, they have my blessing (not that they need it). Instead, my concern with The Shift is a worry that it doesn't work, or at least that it has a flaw that needs fixing.

The data show that while The Shift does a decent job of preventing singles on balls in play (what it's supposed to do), it also increases the number of walks that happen in front of it, and the number of additional walks outweighs the number of singles saved. It's a problem because you can't throw a guy out if he gets to walk to first base.

But the "why" was important. It seemed that The Shift was changing the way in which pitchers pitched. We saw that there were fewer fastballs thrown in front of The Shift than we might otherwise expect, and that pitchers tended to stay out of the strike zone a little more. Not by a lot. In fact, it might not even be visible to the naked eye. The percentage of pitches that are out of the zone goes from 51.0 to 53.3 from a standard defense (two right/two left) to a full shift (three on one side). That difference stands up even after we control for the types of hitters that get shifted against. And it's enough to drive up the walk rate to where it cancels out the benefits that teams thought they were getting with The Shift… and then some.

But there was some hope. I found that when individual pitchers stayed closer to the in-zone/out-of-zone mix that they used without The Shift on, they could still get the benefits of The Shift without the walk problems. So, in theory, a team could simply figure out a way to convince its pitchers to not fall prey to the walk trap and The Shift would once again be their friend.

It's reasonable to think that some teams might be more hip to this idea than others. Maybe some figured it out a year before the others. Maybe they were better at getting the message across to their pitchers. Or, maybe no one has figured it out yet.

Warning! Gory Mathematical Details Ahead!

I used data from 2015-2017, made available through MLB's data portal, Baseball Savant. They are kind enough to note when teams are using an infield shift (three fielders on one side of second base), as opposed to a "strategic shift" (someone's playing a bit out of position, but it's not quite that drastic) or a "standard" alignment.

Since we're doing this by team, I can't just look at raw walk rates, because we know that some teams have good pitchers and others have not-so-good pitchers. Some have a mix of both. I used the log-odds ratio method to take into account a batter's general walking proclivities, and a pitcher's as well, and then shoving them into a binary logistic regression. Then, I asked the computer to generate a specific coefficient for each team's pitchers, for when they went into The Shift and how that affected their walk rate.

Using those coefficients, I was able to project what would happen if a league-average pitcher faced a league-average hitter (which we expect would product a league-average walk rate; from 2015-2017, 7.7 percent of plate appearances ended in a walk) and then just switched his hat. Here's the top five and the bottom five:

Top 5 Teams	Projected Shift Walk Rate	Bottom 5 Teams	Projected Shift Walk Rate
Rockies	6.2%	Rangers	11.2%
Pirates	6.7%	Mets	10.4%
Indians	7.2%	Dodgers	10.2%
Astros	7.3%	Cardinals	9.9%
Braves	7.7%	Tigers	9.7%

There are probably people out there right now trying to figure out what the common thread is among the top and bottom teams. I'm sure, because this is Baseball Prospectus, people are already trying to make the case that sabermetric "early adopters" have some sort of edge here. I think that the more interesting piece is that by the time you get to fifth place in The Shift, we're at league average.

As a sanity check, I examined the issue on a pitch-by-pitch level, looking at how often pitchers threw their pitches in the GameDay strike zone, and again using the same basic methodology and getting team-specific coefficients. The names on the list re-arranged themselves, but the idea was the same, and the two lists correlated with an R of .593.

There's a reason that I don't usually do this type of leaderboard post. I don't really know what the Rockies, Pirates, Indians, Astros, and Braves have in common, or what they have that the bottom five don't. I can put a shrug emoji here and say, "Well, it must be something!" but that seems like a cop-out. Instead, I'd like to present another table and suggest that the table above doesn't even really matter anymore.

Year	League Percent Outside K Zone (Full Shift)	League Percent in K Zone (No Shift)	Difference
2015	54.1%	51.1%	3.0%
2016	53.3%	50.9%	2.4%
2017	52.6%	50.9%	1.7%
2018	52.0%	50.7%	1.3%

The hole in The Shift is fixing itself, and it's coming down really fast league wide. In my earlier work on The Shift, I suggested that until teams stopped having such a huge difference between their out-of-zone rate with and without The Shift on, there would just be too many walks for The Shift to make sense. It seems that all 30 of them have been working toward just that. I once estimated that it takes about 10 years for an idea to filter its way through baseball. At this rate, it looks like teams are going to catch up a lot faster than that. And yeah, they're all saber-smart now.

It's likely that whatever magic it was that the Rockies and Pirates had has made its way to Texas and Queens. Or is at least on its way. And if teams are committing to fixing the walk problem, then it's likely that they will continue shifting and shifting a lot.

And eventually it's going to actually make sense for them to do it.

—*Russell Carleton is a former author of Baseball Prospectus and now an analyst for the New York Mets.*

The State of the Quality Start

Rob Mains

One of the seven things you (probably) didn't know about the 2018 season is that quality starts—defined as a start lasting six or more innings with three or fewer earned runs allowed—as a percentage of total starts cratered to an all-time low of 41 percent. I want to look a little more deeply into this, since it's been a while (May of 2016, to be exact) since I've examined quality starts.

The term *quality start* is credited to *Philadelphia Inquirer* sportswriter John Lowe. It's been derided ever since he coined it in December of 1985. Three runs in six innings? That's a 4.50 ERA! In what world is that a measure of quality?

Let's start with that criticism. It's true that 3 x 9 / 6 = 4.5. (You came here for this sort of high-level math, right?) But it's also true that type of start, meeting the bare minimum for earning a quality start, is unusual. Here's the proportion of quality starts in which the pitcher lasted exactly six innings and yielded exactly three earned runs. (I'm going to confine this analysis to the 30-team era, 1998-present. Almost all data retrieved in this article is via the Baseball-Reference Play Index.)

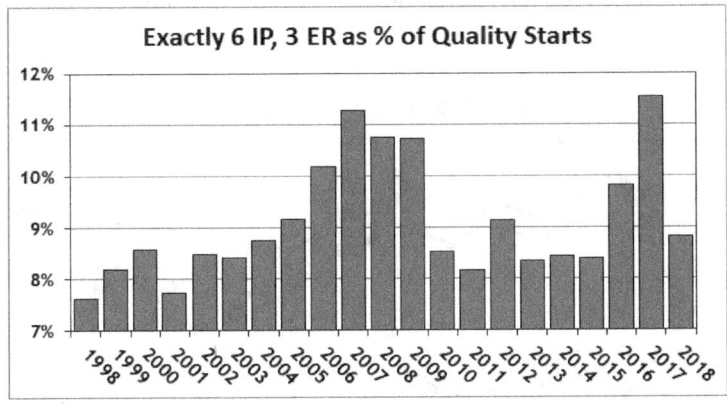

There were 1,997 quality starts in 2018. Only 176, or fewer than one in 11, featured a pitcher going six innings and allowing three earned runs. Put another way, the percentage of quality starts that resulted in a 4.50 ERA (8.8 percent) is less than half the percentage of games in which a batter hit two home runs and his team lost (22.5 percent; 237-69 won-lost). That doesn't impugn hitting two homers.

So if a 4.50 ERA isn't the norm, what is? How good are quality starts? Pretty good, it turns out. First, on a team level:

Teams receiving a quality start from their pitcher won 68.4 percent of their games in 2018, in line with the 30-team era average of 67.9 percent. A team with a .684 winning percentage wins 111 games. Getting a quality start is definitely a good thing. Individual pitchers throwing quality starts have a higher winning percentage because a big slice of team losses is assigned to a reliever.

If teams do well in quality starts, how well do the starting pitchers do? Again, very well.

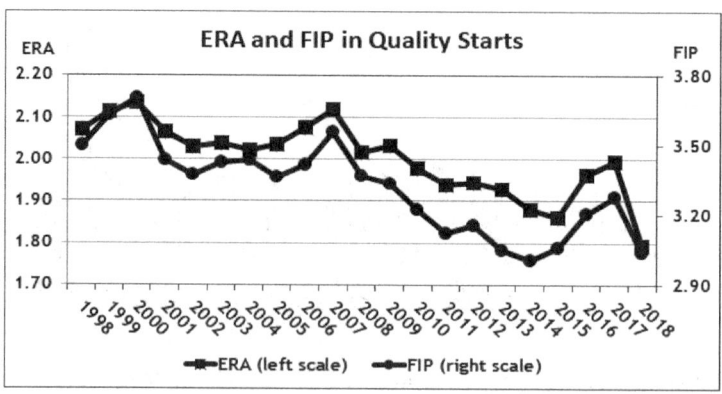

Pitchers in quality starts had a 1.79 ERA (blue line) in 2018, *the lowest in the 30-team era*. Their FIP was higher, 3.04, but still excellent. In the 30-team era, only 2014 had a lower FIP for quality starts, 3.01.

But, of course, the run environment in 2014 was different. Teams in 2014 scored 4.07 runs per game, the fewest in a non-strike year since 1976. They scored 4.45 runs per game in 2018. So surrendering a 3.04 FIP in 2018 is more impressive than 3.01 in 2014. Accordingly, let's look at ERA and FIP in quality starts relative to league averages.

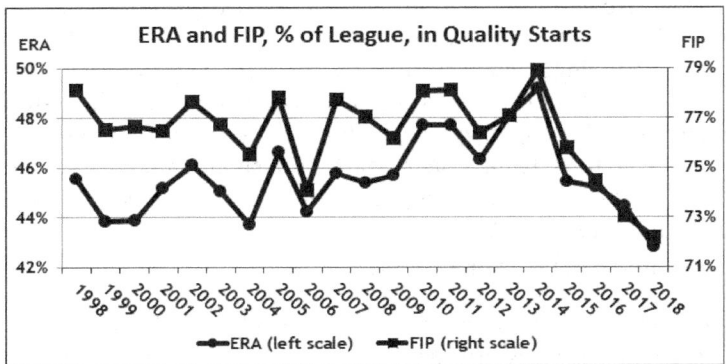

This tells a more dramatic story. Starting pitchers in 2018 gave up a 4.19 ERA and a 4.21 FIP. Starters in quality starts gave up a 1.79 ERA, 43 percent of the league average. Starters in quality starts gave up a 3.04 FIP, 72 percent of the league average. Both of these marks represent lows in the 30-team era.

The takeaway here is this: *Quality starts are better, relative to other starts, than they've ever been over the past 21 years.*

Maybe during the winter I'll look at this over a longer arc of time. For now, though, we can definitively say quality starts are the best they've ever been since the Diamondbacks and Rays joined the majors.

Yet, paradoxically, they're down.

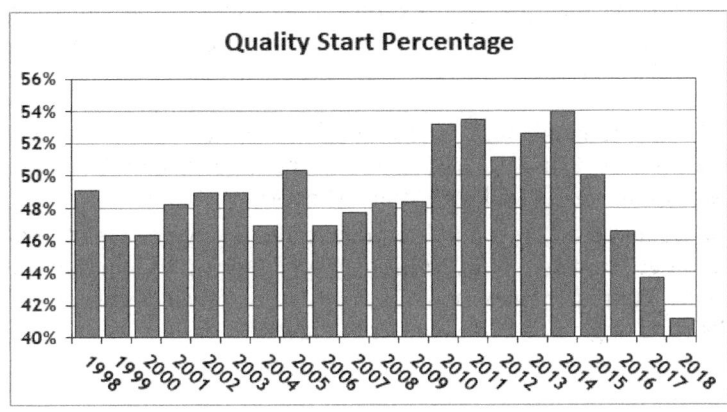

This graph covers only the 30-team era. In my article last week, though, I looked at the years 1908-2018. The result was the same. The 41 percent of starts in 2018 that were quality starts are an all-time low, well below the runners-up: 1930's 43 percent (the year teams scored an all-time record 5.55 runs per game) and last year's 44 percent.

The normal explanation for a dip in quality start percentage is an increase in scoring. When teams score a lot of runs, it's harder for starting pitchers to last six or more innings and limit opponents to three earned runs. From 1998 to 2014, the correlation between runs scored per game and the percentage of starts that were quality starts was -0.94. That means there was an extremely close relationship: More runs, fewer quality starts. Too small a sample? Go back to the start of the Expansion Era, 1961, and the relationship is even more negative, a -0.95 correlation, though 2014.

But that's broken down over the past four years:

- 2015: Runs per game increased from 4.07 to 4.25, quality start percentage decreased from 54.0 to 50.1. Yes, that's a negative relationship, but the regression model would predict a decline of 1.5 percentage points. We got 3.9 instead.
- 2016: Runs per game increased from 4.25 to 4.48, quality start percentage decreased from 50.1 to 46.6. Past experience would suggest a decline of just 1.8 percentage points. We got 3.4.
- 2017: Runs per game increased from 4.48 to 4.65, quality start percentage decreased from 46.6 to 43.6. Again, the direction's right, but the magnitude isn't. Using the relationship from 1998 to 2014, that increase in scoring should've reduced quality starts by 1.3 percentage points, not 2.9.
- 2018: Runs per game declined from 4.65 to 4.45. That should've resulted in the quality start percentage moving in the other direction, rising 1.6 points. It didn't. It fell 2.6 points, as noted, to an all-time low.

Granted, we're talking about just four years here. Maybe they're outliers. But I don't think they are. Quality starts, as noted, are as good or better than ever. But they're rarer than ever as well. And I think I know why.

To get a quality start, you need to allow three or fewer earned and pitch at least six innings. That's 18 outs. Here's a graph showing the number of starting pitchers who limited their opponents to three or fewer earned runs but got pulled after pitching at least five innings but fewer than six:

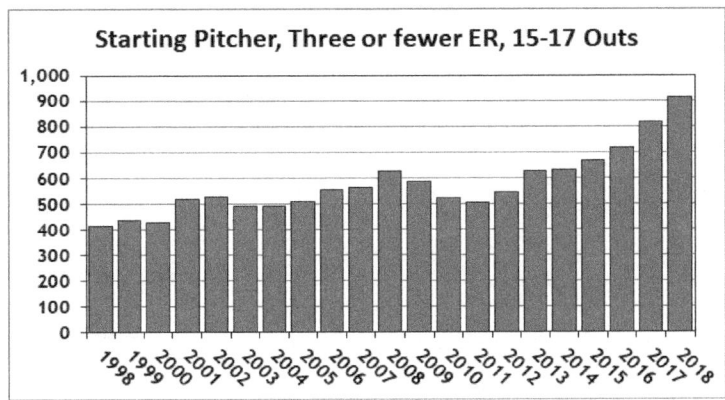

A pitcher getting 15 outs pitched five innings. A pitcher getting 16 outs pitched 5 1/3. A pitcher getting 17 outs pitched 5 2/3. More than ever before, pitchers are being removed from games in which they are within 1-3 outs of a quality start, falling just short of the six-inning finish line. Widespread acknowledgement of the times-through-the-order penalty and a flotilla of available bullpen arms is making the quality start simultaneously both more excellent and more rare.

Which is ironic, given that we saw a new post-war quality start record this season:

Rank	Pitcher	Season	Consecutive QS
1	Jacob deGrom	2018	24
2	Bob Gibson	1968	22
-	Chris Carpenter	2005	22
4	Johan Santana	2004	21
5	Luis Tiant	1968	20
-	Mike Scott	1986	20
-	Jake Arrieta	2015	20
8	Robin Roberts	1952	19
-	Tom Seaver	1973	19
-	Jack Morris	1983	19
-	Greg Maddux	1998	19
-	Josh Johnson	2010	19
-	Jon Lester	2014	19

While there have been longer streaks spread over multiple seasons, no pitcher since World War II threw more consecutive quality starts in one year than Jacob deGrom this year. The fact that he did in a year in which quality starts were the rarest they've ever been adds to the accomplishment.

—Rob Mains is an author of Baseball Prospectus.

Heads-Up Hacking—The First Pitch

Matthew Trueblood

Batters fell behind in a higher percentage of all plate appearances in 2018 than in any previous season for which we have pitch-by-pitch data. That kind of granular information goes back only to 1988, but we might safely assume (given all we know about baseball as it had been before that, and as it has been in the years since) that batters have *never* fallen behind at a higher rate than they did last season.

Through the 1990s, the percentage of all plate appearances that began 0-1 hovered in the high 30s and low 40s. In the 2000s, it rose steadily but slowly, through the mid-40s. In 2018, 49.8 percent of all trips to the plate began 0-1. That, as much as anything, captures in microcosm the nature of hitting in MLB today.

A countdown clock toward strike three begins ticking almost the moment a batter takes his place in the box. The league's adjusted OPS+ on the first pitch was higher in 2018 than ever before, and that has been true in most of the last 10 seasons. Batters hit .264/.289/.442 in all plate appearances in which they swung at the first pitch last season, and .241/.330/.395 in all plate appearances in which they took that first offering.

The percentage differences in batting average and isolated power there favor swinging at the first pitch by more than in any season since 1988, while the difference in on-base percentage favors taking by more than ever. If you want to get on base at a decent clip, it's a good idea to be patient, but you run the risk of missing the only chances you'll get to produce power.

Baltimore Orioles 2019

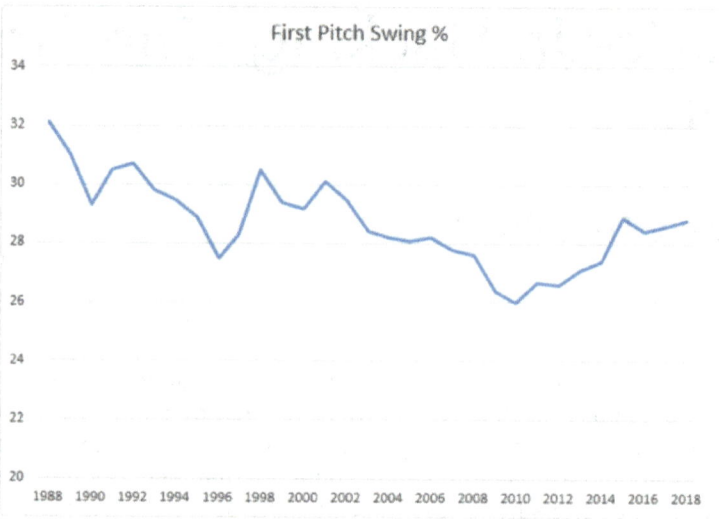

The league swung at the first pitch 28.8 percent of the time in 2018. With the isolated exception of 2015, that's the highest that number has climbed since 2002, but it might not be high enough. With the help of BP research maven Rob McQuown, I looked at the aggregate Called Strike Probability (CSProb) on the first pitch for each season since 2008, when the implementation of PITCHf/x first made measuring that possible. It's risen sharply during that period.

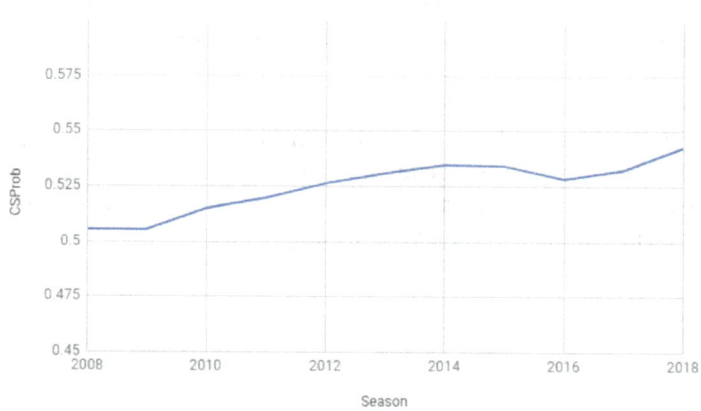

Called Strike Probability, First Pitch of PA (2008-2018)

Called Strike Probability is exactly what it sounds like: a pitch with a given CSProb has roughly that chance of being called a strike, if not swung at. In 2018, a batter who took 100 first pitches from a random sampling of the league's pitchers might expect to fall behind 54 or 55 times—up from 50 or 51 times in 2008. Almost regardless of pitch type (and, notably, especially in the case of fastballs), the first pitch tends to have more of the zone right now than ever before.

Pitchers are better at throwing strikes. They have better stuff, and believe more in their ability to miss bats within the zone. Perhaps most importantly, they know that batters are looking for one thing on the first pitch: a fastball. If they don't get it, they're likely to take the pitch. Check out how the use of sinkers and four-seamers on the first pitch has changed in a decade:

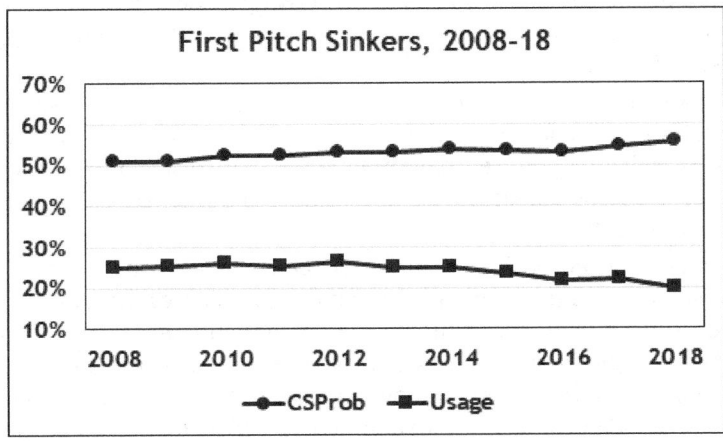

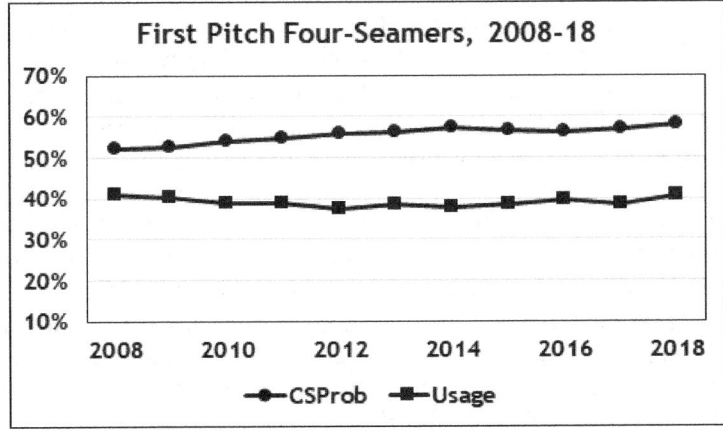

Baltimore Orioles 2019

The sinker is losing its place in baseball, but the rate at which pitchers have thrown it on the first pitch hasn't dropped any faster than its usage rate in other counts. Pitchers have actually gone to their four-seamer *more* often to open counts, in the last few years, after a dip in the 2012-2015 period. What's really changed, though, and what shows up in both charts above, is that pitchers are catching more of the zone with first-pitch fastballs than they were a decade ago, or a half-decade ago. They're attacking right away, even with the pitch they know batters are expecting. The message is pretty clear: batters are being too passive.

Sliders, curves, and changeups each have more of the zone when thrown on the first pitch than they did several years ago, too, though the effect is less pronounced. Pitchers have seen the numbers; they know batters are doing better on the first pitch itself. They still feel safe throwing more and better strikes than ever before, figuring they'll come out ahead as long as they keep getting ahead to open each battle.

The Moneyball revolution brought an increased league-wide focus on OBP, which resulted in a de facto mandate to take a more patient tack at the plate. It worked very well for a while, as batters with poor plate discipline were compelled to either adjust or be expelled from the league, and pitchers with poor control were slowly weeded out.

However, concurrent with that revolution, and spurred by it in some ways, was the evolution of the pitching paradigm that now dominates the game. As batters ratcheted up their focus on inflating pitch counts and working walks, pitchers honed theirs on throwing strikes and missing bats. The league's understanding of what makes a good pitcher improved at least as much, from the mid-1990s through the mid-2000s, as its understanding of what makes a good hitter. As amphetamines and other performance-enhancing drugs were phased mostly out of the game, and as PITCHf/x broke onto the scene, individuals and teams learned how to exploit the evolved approaches of even the smartest hitters.

The ability to avoid making outs is still the most valuable one in baseball, but the magnitude of its eclipse of slugging is smaller than ever. To a greater extent than power, on-base skills derive their value from chaining—from the on-base skill levels of the players on either side of a given individual. Eleven years ago, when the housing crisis hit, people learned the hard way that the value of their homes depended a good deal on the values of their neighbors' homes. The same wasn't true, though, of their cars. So it is now, with OBP and SLG.

The global OBP in 2018 was .318. The only seasons since the Dead Ball Era in which the league got on base at a worse clip were 2013-2015, 1988, 1971-1972, and 1963-1968. This is all happening despite the aforementioned evolution of the science of hitting. It's happening despite a shift in approach and focus, one that would steer OBP ever higher, if only it were working.

Instead, it's sitting at a low ebb, and while it does so, even guys who get on base often are a little less helpful than they were 10 years ago—or 20, or 40, or 60, or 70, or 80, or 90. They're less helpful, that is, because unless there happen to be three or four other guys in the lineup who get on just as regularly, their contribution is merely to forestall the inevitable. Runs happen, increasingly, when a sudden bang happens, and that means attacking early in the count—because pitchers are sure as hell doing that.

In a league making contact on barely 75 percent of its swings, and a league in which an increasing number of pitchers can throw multiple off-speed pitches for strikes in any count, the only way to consistently generate offense is going to be aggressive. This isn't necessarily true for individuals, like Mookie Betts and Jose Ramirez, who make a lot of contact and have excellent plate discipline, and whose power comes from such natural quickness in a short stroke. Most players have to make tradeoffs, though, whether it be lowering their contact rate or raising their chase rate, in order to consistently make the quality of contact necessary to survive in today's game.

Highest %	Lowest %
Javier Baez – 48.3	Joe Mauer – 4.6
Freddie Freeman – 47.1	Mookie Betts – 9.7
Ozzie Albies – 46.3	Brett Gardner – 10.7
Jose Altuve – 44.2	Jose Ramirez – 12.0
Nick Castellanos – 44.1	Jason Kipnis – 13.8
Joey Gallo – 42.3	Jesus Aguilar – 14.5
Corey Dickerson – 40.9	Xander Bogaerts – 15.8
Salvador Perez – 40.8	Brian Dozier – 16.3
Eddie Rosario – 40.7	Mike Trout – 17.6
Nick Ahmed – 40.4	Yasmani Grandal – 17.6

Top 10 and Bottom 10 Hitters, First-Pitch Swing Rate (2018)

The question isn't which of these lists one prefers, but what they each convey, qualitatively, about the cat-and-mouse game of early-count hitting. Those top five on the left, especially, drive home the fact that for most players, getting aggressive early in the count is now key to keeping strikeout rate down and hitting for power.

For now, the message is: pitchers are coming right after batters with the nastiest stuff they've ever had. Batters had better stop giving away strike one and force hurlers to adjust, or the global OBP crisis is only going to get worse.

—*Matthew Trueblood is an author of Baseball Prospectus.*

A Hymn for the Index Stat

Patrick Dubuque

We survived without computers. I know this, because I remember the day when my dad hooked up his brand-new Atari 400 computer to the back of our 12-inch Magnavox television, and the perfect blue of the memo pad lit up for the first time. I was born just on the edge of that transitional generation, of learning cursive and balancing checkbooks and just doing math all the time, constant manual arithmetic.

It still amazes me. We learned how to sail ships without computers. We learned how to do calculus. We built towers that didn't fall down, most of the time. We engineered catapults to knock them down anyway. We built a robust system of philosophy called "utilitarianism," founded on the principle that the good of an action is evaluated by summing the effects of that action, which is the kind of formula that would make the world's mainframes crash. The whole foundation of statistics as a field is "here's math you could easily do but would die of old age first."

The fact of the matter is that there is too much math in the world to do. There are too many things changing, and too many things too small to notice, for us to handle. At some point, they become too much for the computers to handle as well, which is why we have chaos theory and undetectable earthquakes, but it's not an even fight. At some point, we fall back on intuition, and given how under-equipped we are, we're forced to bestow that intuition with some sort of supernatural superiority, the "gut feeling," that we can't prove because we can only intuit that our intuition is better.

We're all lousy at intuition, and wonderful at lying to ourselves about it. The honest truth is that computers are far better at intuition than we are, because in order to know what feels "off" you have to know what's "on." In order to do that you have to constantly reassess the average of everything, then re-rank your own experience against it.

Test your own, by comparing these three anonymous lines:

Player	G	HR	AVG	OBP	SLG
Player A	156	38	.259	.342	.535
Player B	154	38	.280	.348	.527
Player C	158	38	.266	.343	.509

These all seem like pretty similar players, right? The second one a touch more batted-ball dependent, the third a little less strong, but all pretty good hitters. And you'd be right, about the latter. Not the former.

Here's the breakdown:

- Player A: 1991 Howard Johnson, 141 DRC+
- Player B: 1996 Dean Palmer, 121 DRC+
- Player C: 2018 Giancarlo Stanton, 114 DRC+

Baseball is fortunate to have escaped the seismic shifts of so many other sports, where the talents and performances of other eras are nearly unrecognizable. (And not just other sports: try to explain the greatness of the movie Duck Soup without adjusting for era.) But they're still there, and they're nearly impossible to account for manually, without having to resort to sweeping generalizations like "steroid era" or juiced-ball era" to throw out entire swathes of production.

This is all to say that we should celebrate the index stat, that simple 100-based scale with such a humble aim: just to give context. It's hard to imagine how we lived without them for so long. Sabermetricians have always tried to make their stats look like other stats: True Average mapped to batting average, FIP molded to look like and compare to ERA. It's easy to understand the motivation—these statistics carry an emotional value in them that is hard to resist, as with the .300 hitter and the 2.00 ERA—but even they fall prey to the same loss of scale as their unadjusted counterparts. If a .300 average means different things in different years, does that hold true for a .300 True Average?

Instead, 100 doesn't say anything, except above average or below. And it does it instantly, for every season in every run environment for any statistic we want it to. We should have more index stats: K%+, so we can stop comparing Mike Clevinger's career 9.46 K/9 to Nolan Ryan's 9.55. HBP%+, so we can note that Ron Hunt was getting plunked when nobody else was getting plunked, as opposed to that imitator Brandon Guyer. Some might note how stale these references are and accuse league-adjustment as a backward-looking drive, and this is true. But we're always looking backward, always comparing the new with the expectations already set. The index stat just forces us to be honest.

There's always resistance to a new statistic, especially one so outwardly simple and so internally complex. We tend to stick with what we know, even in the case of formulas that are supposed to tell us what we know. But if your resistance is that it seems too complicated, too counterintuitive, too "black boxy," I encourage you to consider why you feel that way. Because the real world is infinitely more complicated than baseball, where all the pitches go in one basic direction and the baserunners are only allowed to travel in four directions. Baseball statistics based on mixed methodology are almost impossibly intricate. So are skyscrapers and automobiles. That's why we have computers—to take the guesswork out of them.

—*Patrick Dubuque is an author of Baseball Prospectus.*

Index of Names

Akin, Keegan 76, 99
Alberto, Hanser 89
Araujo, Pedro 92
Bannon, Rylan 66
Baumann, Michael 92, 104
Bishop, Cameron 77
Bleier, Richard 42
Bostick, Chris 89
Bundy, Dylan 44
Carmona, Jean 89
Carroll, Cody 46
Cashner, Andrew 48
Castro, Miguel 50
Cobb, Alex 52
Cumberland, Brett 89, 103
Davis, Chris 22
Diaz, Yusniel 67, 95
Encarnacion, Jean Carlos 68, 101
Erwin, Tyler 92
Escobar, Alcides 24
Fenter, Gray 92
Fry, Paul 92
Gilmartin, Sean 92
Givens, Mychal 54
Grenier, Cadyn 69, 103
Hall, Adam 89, 102
Hall, DL 78, 96
Hanifee, Brenan 79
Harvey, Hunter 80, 105
Hays, Austin 70, 100
Hess, David 56
Jackson, Drew 89
Karns, Nate 81
Kline, Branden 92
Knight, Blaine 82
Kremer, Dean 83, 104
Lowther, Zac 84, 102
Mancini, Trey 26
Martin, Richie 89
McKenna, Ryan 71, 98
Mountcastle, Ryan 72, 96
Mullins, Cedric 28
Nunez, Renato 30
Ortiz, Luis 85, 100
Perez, Carlos 89
Peterson, Jace 89
Phillips, Evan 92
Pop, Zach 86, 104
Ramirez, Yefrey 58
Reinheimer, Jack 89
Rickard, Joey 89
Rodriguez, Grayson 87, 97
Rogers, Josh 92
Ruiz, Rio 73
Santander, Anthony 89
Schultz, Bo 92
Scott, Tanner 60
Sisco, Chance 32
Smith, Dwight 89
Stewart, D.J. 74, 104
Sucre, Jesus 89
Susac, Andrew 89

Baltimore Orioles 2019

Tate, Dillon 88, 98
Trumbo, Mark 34
Vielma, Engelb 75
Villar, Jonathan 36
Wells, Alex 92, 103
Wilkerson, Stephen 38
Wright, Mike 62
Wynns, Austin 40
Yacabonis, Jimmy 64
Ynoa, Gabriel 92
Young, Eric 89
Zimmermann, Bruce 102

Ballpark diagrams for Baseball Prospectus are created by THIRTY81Project, a design concept offering original ballpark artwork, including the new 'Ballparks of 2019' 11 x 17 color print.

Visit **www.thirty81project.com** for full details.

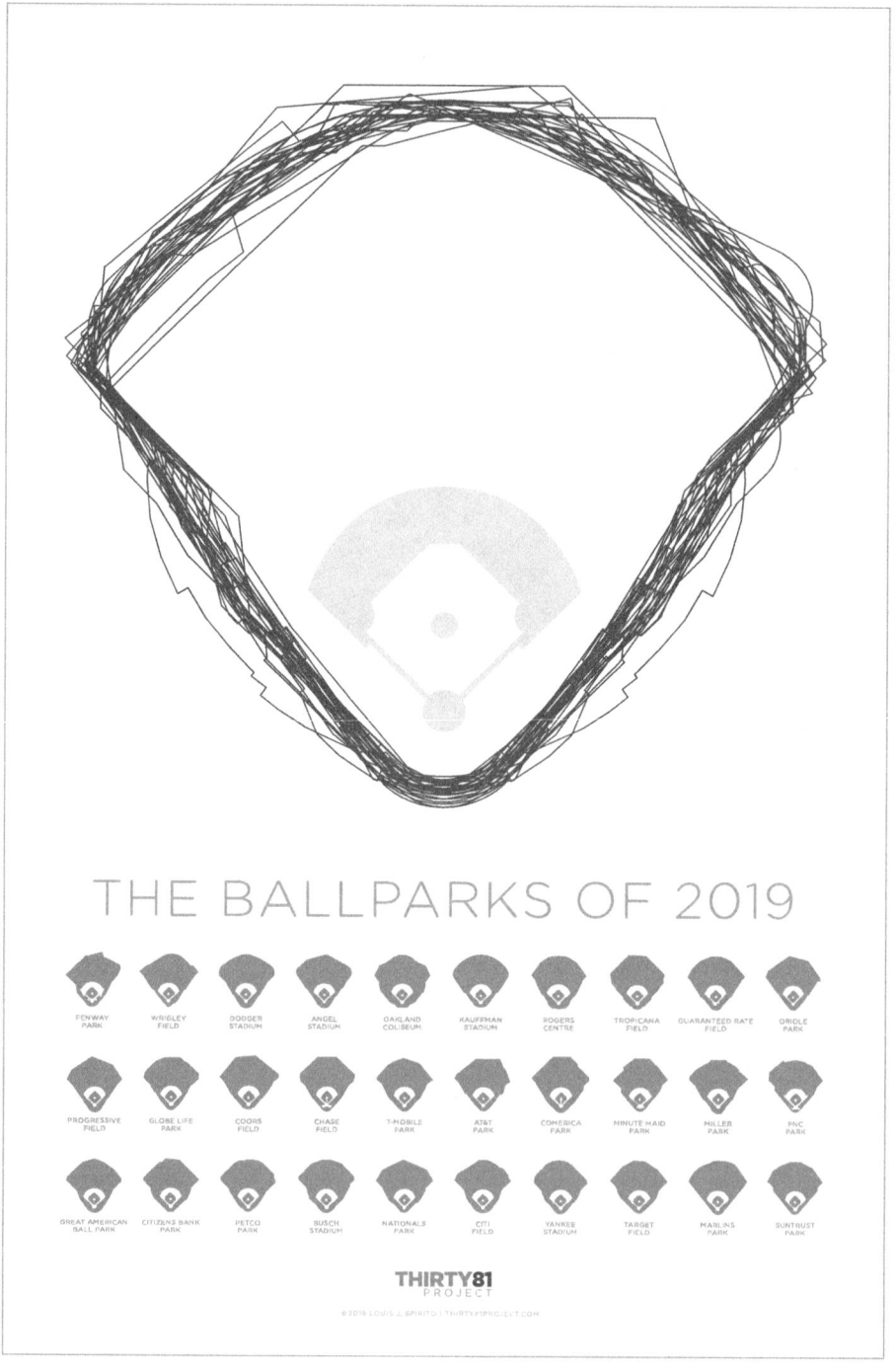